BITCOIN IS F*CK YOU MONEY

THE BRUTALLY HONEST CASE FOR BITCOIN AND FINANCIAL FREEDOM

NICK ALOISIO

"Slavery was never abolished, it was only extended to include all the colors."

— CHARLES BUKOWSKI

CONTENTS

*Preface: It Must be Freedom for All, or Freedom
for None*   9
Introduction   13

1. YOU WERE LIED TO   17
   The Illusion of Wealth and Safety   18
   The System Was Never Built for You   19
   Inflation Is the Quiet Thief   22
   Debt Is the Trap   24
   Bitcoin: The Exit Route from Debt   26
   The Hard Numbers: How Bitcoin Compares   28

2. WHAT IS F*CK YOU MONEY?   31
   Redefining Wealth and Freedom   31
   Why You've Been Trained to Depend on the
   System   34
   The Psychology of F*ck You Money   36
   Why Bitcoin Is the Only True F*ck You Money   39

3. BITCOIN IS DIFFERENT   43
   Why Bitcoin Is Not Crypto   43
   Bitcoin Is Digital Gold—But Stronger   45
   Bitcoin Is Better Than Real Estate   45
   How Bitcoin Actually Works (Without Tech
   Overload)   48
   Bitcoin Is Engineered for Freedom   51
   This Is Not a Trend — This Is the New Base
   Layer   53

4. HOW TO GET STARTED   57
   Buying Bitcoin Without Getting Burned   57
   Where to Keep It — Wallets 101   60
   Mistakes Newbies Always Make   63
   Building Real Conviction   67
   Insights from Thought Leaders   67
   Long-Term Perspective   68

Diligent Inquisition   69
The Resilience of Conviction   69

5. THE WEALTH STRATEGY   71
The Power of Hodling   71
Time in the Market Beats Timing the Market   74
Why "Never Sell" Makes Sense   76
Your Exit Plan Is No Exit   78

6. THE GREATEST WEALTH TRANSFER IN
HISTORY   83
The Ticking Clock   83
The Institutional and Nation-State Space Race   86
The Broken Fiat Machine Can't Keep Up   88
Why You're Still Early — But Not for Long   90

7. BITCOIN CHANGES YOU   93
Bitcoin and Low Time Preference   93
Bitcoin and Responsibility   96
Bitcoin and Mental Clarity   98
Bitcoin as a Spiritual Shift   101

8. A NEW SYSTEM IS ALREADY EMERGING   105
The Rise of Parallel Economies   105
Bitcoin and the End of Financial Surveillance   108
Embracing the Freedom to Innovate   111
Revolutionizing Content Creation   113
Democratization of Innovation   114
Ripple Effects Across Industries   115
Cultivating a Culture of Self-Reliance   116
Redefining Creator and Consumer Interaction   117
Reflecting on Your Role   118
Building a World You Want to Live In   119

9. START TODAY OR STAY STUCK   123
Stop Waiting for Permission   123
How to Start — Safely and Simply   127
Learn More, Trust Less   128
The Life on the Other Side   130
Planning For the Future with Bitcoin   131
Bitcoin as a Guiding Compass   132

Embracing the Future Today   132
Transitioning to Practical Steps   133

10. VISUAL PROOF – BITCOIN VS. THE SYSTEM   135
Chart 1: Global Fiat Collapses and Systemic
Breakdowns (1923–2021)   136
Chart 2: Wages vs. Cost of Living (U.S.)   137
Chart 3: M2 Money Supply Expansion (2008–
2023)   138
Chart 4: Bitcoin vs. Fiat Money Supply (Halving
Comparison)   139
Chart 5: DCA vs. Trading vs. Fiat Saving vs.
S&P 500   140
Chart 6: Internet Adoption vs. Bitcoin Adoption
Curve   141
Chart 7: Platform Censorship vs. Bitcoin's
Censorship Resistance   142
Chart 8: Bitcoin vs. Traditional Assets –
Cumulative Returns   143
Chart 9: Bitcoin in Collapsing Fiat Economies   144
Chart 10: Bitcoin vs. USD Drawdowns
(Volatility vs. Fiat Decay)   145
Chart 11: Custody Risk Spectrum   146
Chart 12: Bitcoin vs. Traditional Assets (2024
Snapshot)   147

Conclusion: The Power to Walk Away   149
Resources for Building Conviction and Taking
Action   153
References   161

PREFACE: IT MUST BE FREEDOM FOR ALL, OR FREEDOM FOR NONE

> *"I don't believe we shall ever have good money again before we take the thing out of the hands of government... all we can do is by some sly roundabout way introduce something that they can't stop."*

> — FRIEDRICH HAYEK, 1984, INTERVIEWED
> BY JAMES U. BLANCHARD III

Writer Andrew Gavin Marshall taught me about Zbigniew Brzezinski's "Great Awakening" through his articles and podcast appearances on FBI whistleblower Sibel Edmonds' blog and podcast network.

Before that, the Iraq War began to wake me up. I signed every anti-war petition there was, however partisan they ended up being in hindsight. I knew there could be consequences to putting my name out there as an anti-war person, but as more of our troops started coming back in flag-draped coffins (that networks weren't allowed to show on the news), my opposition grew to a point where I didn't care. Eventually, my mail stopped showing up, then would arrive months later in packages marked "Address unknown," which the USPS could not explain. Later, I read that some mail was indeed held and inspected by the Bush/Cheney administration.

When Barack Obama bailed out the banks while millions lost their homes, started his own wars, neglected to close Guantanamo, prosecuted whistleblowers, and signed an indefinite detention bill, I knew we were in serious trouble. Occupy Wall Street spoke to me, and I attended a few marches. When Obama gathered the mayors together to coordinate the violent destruction of OWS encampments, I knew the coffin was nailed. Instead of offering us hope, Obama's presidency obliterated it. It became obvious to me that both parties were complicit.

Along with my loss of hope for the future of our republic and the world at large, I saw no path to retirement for myself. I saved as much as I could, but it was nowhere near the amount that all the retirement calculators recommended. I thought I was doomed to work until I was dead.

A 2012 article by Marshall included the refrain "It's either freedom for all or freedom for none." That phrase resonated with me, and the piece awakened me to the concept of direct democracy. He wrote about how technology will either free or enslave us all, forever. I knew he was right, and I began to watch for the technology that could start to set us free from rising authoritarianism. I couldn't envision it, but I was fascinated and once again hopeful.

In 2021, I was watching a YouTube interview with Max Keiser, where he discussed Bitcoin as "freedom money." I was instantly curious. I had no idea this was exactly what I had been waiting for, but it turned out to be precisely that: a peaceful revolution whose time had come. Its built-in game theory benefits the unbanked, workers, executives, corporations, governments, and institutions alike. And I'm not sure that even to this day, Marshall knows that what he predicted already existed at the time, or that he would even agree that Bitcoin is that technology.

I started listening to Max and his wife, Stacy, talk about Bitcoin. The idea that attracted me the most was that Bitcoin will eventually stop war. Because, on a Bitcoin Standard, if our supply of money is capped, they can't just print money every time they want a war. They will need to tax us for it. And eventually, the people will say "no" to taxation for foreign wars of choice for profit, especially at the expense of needs here at home.

In one of the first episodes of their *Orange Pill Podcast* that I listened to, Max mentioned Michael Saylor's existential philosophical perspective, and I was instantly curious.

I found Saylor's extended interview episodes on the *What Is Money?* podcast, and I was hooked. From that day forward, I knew this was the answer to both my retirement problem and so many of the world's issues. I had to buy as much Bitcoin as I could. I began to think about it day and night, and, to this day, I can't keep my eyes off the price, which has more than tripled since then, despite its extreme volatility, once dipping more than 50%.

I view this book, along with the other Bitcoin-related books I've written, as a gift to people like me who have felt hopeless about the future, retirement, or even surviving their golden years. Parents, you don't need to worry, the kids are alright. And to the students, you are lucky. There is more than hope. There is assurance. You can survive. You can beat the system before it beats you. You have Bitcoin. You don't need much, but it might be best to start buying now, while it's still relatively cheap compared to where it's headed.

"The interesting fact is that never before in human history have either of these processes been truly possible until today: global domination or global liberation. Both, moreover, are advanced by the same socially transformative process: the Technological Revolution. This is the modern form of the historical human revolutions which brought about the Stone Age and organized human society. In this context, humanity is now emerging from its historical adolescence, where we have always had, and to some degree required, some form of authority telling us how to think, what to do, how to act, who to be; but now, it is time to become an adult: to become autonomous, free, independent, and liberated. It must be freedom for all, or freedom for none."

— ANDREW GAVIN MARSHALL, IT MUST BE
FREEDOM FOR ALL, OR FREEDOM FOR
NONE, FEB 15, 2012

INTRODUCTION

"You are not machines. You are not cattle. You are men. You have the love of humanity in your hearts."

— CHARLIE CHAPLIN, THE GREAT
DICTATOR (1940)

You played by the rules. You worked hard, saved diligently, and trusted the system. Yet here you are — watching your money lose value, carrying debt, and questioning the promises that were supposed to secure your future.

This isn't a personal failure. It's a structural problem. The system wasn't built to reward your effort but to keep you dependent.

That's where "F*ck You Money" comes in. It's not just about wealth. It's about freedom. The power to say no. The ability to live on your own terms. Bitcoin makes that possible. Not because it's magic, but because it's engineered differently — for you, not against you.

The urgency is real. Inflation quietly drains your savings. Debt loads break records. Government narratives gaslight you into thinking everything's fine — until it isn't. Remember when the U.S. confiscated gold? If they did it once, they can do it again. Your wealth isn't safe if it's not truly yours.

Bitcoin is different. It's decentralized. Scarce. Transparent. It doesn't answer to governments, banks, or central planners. It can't be inflated, seized, or censored. It's not just a digital asset — it's a new foundation for personal sovereignty.

This book is for the disillusioned, the skeptical, the curious. People who've worked hard but feel stuck. People who suspect the game is rigged — and want out. You're not crazy. You're not alone.

My story mirrors yours. I was a software product manager doing everything "right," but something didn't add up. Raises hardly kept up with the real cost of living. The deeper I looked, the more obvious it became — this system wasn't designed to help people like me get ahead. Any progress I made was erased by inflation. Bitcoin didn't just offer hope — it provided a way to take back control.

At first, I was a little skeptical. Was this too good to be true? How could it not be a secret spy operation designed to suck us in and steal everything we owned? But the more I studied, the clearer it became: this wasn't hype. It was an opportunity — and a responsibility.

This book isn't about trends or trading. It's about building conviction, protecting wealth, and living free. You'll learn why "never sell" is more than a meme — it's a strategy. Why borrowing against Bitcoin can be smarter than cashing out. Why this moment in history matters — and why you still have time to act.

This is your outline. Your challenge. Your signal to move.

Don't wait for permission. Don't wait for the system to collapse. Start with what you have and where you are, and build from there. Bitcoin is F*ck You Money — and your journey to financial sovereignty starts now.

CHAPTER 1
YOU WERE LIED TO

"The modern theory of the perpetuation of debt has drenched the Earth with blood and crushed its inhabitants under burdens ever accumulating."

— THOMAS JEFFERSON

S tanding in line at the grocery store, you notice a security guard by the entrance. You can't help but wonder — when did buying food start requiring protection? Just down the street, a once-busy strip mall sits half-empty, its windows boarded and tagged with graffiti.

These aren't dystopian hypotheticals — this is everyday America. And while the cracks in the system are now impossible to ignore, many still pretend that "normal" is just around the corner. But what if it never was?

What if everything you believed about security, stability, and success was a carefully packaged illusion? What if the system was never built to reward your effort — just to keep you compliant?

The Illusion of Wealth and Safety

In Brentwood, California, luxury SUVs glide past manicured hedges, while just beyond the gates, tents mushroom along sidewalks and freeway ramps. It's not a fluke. Homeless encampments now dot suburban neighborhoods across the country, places that once symbolized safety and success.

The image is jarring: the rich behind walls, the poor at the fence. This isn't some distant third-world disparity — it's here. What we once pitied from afar now unfolds outside our front doors. We've become what we used to fear.

These scenes aren't isolated. They're symptoms. Symptoms of a system stretched to its limit — of a promise broken. Once-thriving strip malls are shuttered. Security guards patrol grocery stores. Stores close earlier, install bars, and mount cameras in every corner.

And yet the illusion persists. People still post vacation photos, still talk about career milestones, still chase "normal" as if it's coming back. But under the surface, everyone feels it: the tension, the instability, the slow unraveling.

You were told this couldn't happen here, that the American dream was built to last. But dreams don't decay — systems do. And this one is showing its seams.

This isn't about panic. It's about clarity. Once you recognize that the system is failing by design — not by accident — you can stop clinging to it. You can choose to exit the illusion and start building something real.

The System Was Never Built for You

The 2008 financial crisis was a stark revelation. It laid bare a truth many suspected but few dared confront: the financial system isn't designed with your best interests in mind. When the dust settled, it wasn't everyday people who were rescued. It was the banks — the very entities whose reckless practices fueled the crisis. Governments rushed to their aid with taxpayer-funded bailouts, effectively rewarding failure while ordinary citizens faced foreclosures and financial ruin.

The rich emerged richer than before, their fortunes intact and even expanded, while the middle class was crushed under the weight of lost homes and evaporated savings. It was a harsh lesson in systemic bias — a game where those at the top always win, and everyone else is left scrambling.

Fiat systems are inherently biased. They favor capital over labor, and they reward those who play with assets — not those who work for a living.

> *"The (United) States is run by the Federal Reserve, an institution that answers only to itself and to a few large banks. It's modelled on the Bank of England. Ben Franklin said that one of the main reasons America revolted was to get away from the Bank of England, the mother of all central banks — the most pernicious and insidious of all."*
>
> — MAX KEISER

Let's call the system by its name: fiat. Fiat money is currency created by governments and declared legal tender — not because it's backed by anything real, but simply because the government says so. "Fiat" is Latin for *let it be done.* It's money by decree, not by value. It can be printed at will. It loses purchasing power over time. And it gives central banks immense control over your economic life.

Policies are designed to extract from workers and concentrate rewards at the top. Insiders protect their own interests while everyone else fights for scraps. The game is rigged — and your role is to keep it going.

It's no wonder you feel uneasy. You've done everything right — earned the degree, landed the job, bought the house. But stability remains elusive. Success feels fragile, not freeing. The dream you were sold promised prosperity, but the reality piles on pressure. The ladder stretches endlessly — with no top in sight.

The pain you feel isn't accidental. It's by design. Inflation eats away at your savings. Debt builds faster than you can pay it down. These aren't system glitches — they're system features. Your struggle is the fuel that keeps the machine running.

And yet, seeing the truth is empowering — because it means you can choose to stop playing their game.

While you work tirelessly to make ends meet, policies crafted behind closed doors prioritize those who already hold wealth and power. It's not paranoia — it's the plan. Even the most diligent end up treading water.

The system isn't broken. It's working exactly as intended. It keeps power consolidated while selling the illusion that hard work leads to wealth. But now, you have an alternative — a way out. Bitcoin offers that escape. It isn't controlled by central banks. It doesn't care where you live, how much you earn, or what credentials you have. It's money you can opt into — and no one can stop you.

If you've felt isolated in your frustration, know this: you're not alone. Millions of others are waking up. They're done chasing rewards in a rigged economy. They're choosing something better.

Understanding this landscape is crucial. It gives you the power to act deliberately — not reactively. To redefine success on your terms. Not the system's. But your own.

This isn't theory. It's happening now. People are walking away from the old game — and toward financial sovereignty.

Bitcoin is the on-ramp. It's not just an asset — it's a statement. A refusal to conform. A declaration that you won't participate in a system engineered to exploit you.

So, ask yourself: Are you ready for a new paradigm? Are you willing to leave behind what no longer serves you?

If the answer is yes — keep going. What comes next isn't just survival.

It's sovereignty.

Inflation Is the Quiet Thief

Inflation is often portrayed as a benign, even necessary, part of economic growth. Official numbers assure us it's "under control," hovering at manageable percentages. But these figures are misleading. They exclude real-world essentials like housing, healthcare, and education — the very categories where prices have surged.

The Consumer Price Index (CPI) conveniently sidesteps these realities, painting a rosier picture for headlines while everyday people feel the squeeze. It's clever propaganda: a façade of stability masking the silent erosion of your purchasing power.

Wages, supposedly reflecting productivity, rarely keep pace. The old promise—that hard work leads to prosperity—has become a hollow slogan. Today, two incomes are required to sustain what one used to provide. The idea of building generational wealth on honest labor feels like a relic. For many, the American dream is fading, and inflation is one of the reasons why.

Governments, under the guise of "stimulating the economy," print money without restraint. Every new dollar dilutes the value of the ones you already hold. That's not growth — that's theft—a tax on your savings, imposed without your consent. More dollars chasing the same goods leads to higher prices. The result? Savers lose. Debtors win. And discipline is punished.

Bitcoin offers a radical alternative. It has a fixed supply — 21 million coins, no more. Politicians or central banks don't set that limit. It's coded, auditable, and enforced by a global network. Bitcoin doesn't inflate. It doesn't bend to policy. It's a digital stronghold in a storm of economic manipulation.

While fiat currencies decay year after year, Bitcoin holds its ground. Its value isn't propped up by trust in institutions. It's protected by code, decentralization, and the mathematical certainty of scarcity. Bitcoin is not just another investment. It's a defense system—a way to protect your future from a machine built to take.

Imagine being able to plan a decade ahead without fearing your savings will be worth less every year. Bitcoin offers that possibility — a sense of financial stability that fiat simply can't match. In a world full of monetary chaos, it offers something rare: predictability.

Inflation isn't just an economic metric. It's a force that shapes your everyday choices. It limits your ability to save, to invest, and to rest. But once you understand how it works — and why it's allowed to continue — you can choose something different.

You don't have to accept erosion as inevitable. By investing in assets that resist debasement, you push back. You shift the balance of power.

Bitcoin's rising adoption reflects this awakening. People aren't just speculating — they're exiting. Quietly, one by one, they're choosing sovereignty over obedience.

So, ask yourself: how has inflation shaped your financial journey? What have you lost to this silent force — time, options, peace of mind? And more importantly, are you ready to fight back?

Bitcoin isn't just money. It's a new relationship with value itself—one built on empowerment, not control. For those willing to make the leap, it offers more than protection—it offers a future.

Are you ready to stop playing by their rules? Because Bitcoin is how you start writing your own.

Debt Is the Trap

Debt holds this entire system together — not stability, not savings, and certainly not trust.

Banks create money by lending what they don't have. It's a magic trick disguised as policy. You take out a loan, and *poof* — new money enters the system. Not earned. Just typed into existence.

They profit. You pay. For decades.

Banks are the puppet masters. Through fractional reserve banking, they create money from thin air. They lend out far more than they actually hold. Every time you take a loan — for a car, a house, or school — you're not just borrowing money. You're helping manufacture it. Debt becomes money, and money becomes chains.

This sleight of hand is immensely profitable — for them. For you, it's decades of repayment. You carry the weight while they skim the upside.

And it gets worse. In this economy, earning more doesn't mean freedom — it often means more access to credit. Higher income leads to lifestyle inflation: bigger homes, luxury cars, "deserved" upgrades. Banks happily enable this with higher limits, better rates, and endless offers.

But those offers are traps dressed as trophies. The more you earn, the more you owe. What looks like success is often a debt-fueled illusion that can collapse with a single job loss or market dip.

The U.S. government is no different. Its national debt climbs every year, borrowing just to pay interest on past borrowing. It's the same trap — just scaled up. An entire system hooked on IOUs, with no intention of paying them back. The burden is pushed to future generations. The collapse is delayed, not avoided.

This is the world fiat built: a world of constant debt, endless promises, and artificial wealth. A world where the system doesn't collapse when you default — you collapse when it does.

Bitcoin breaks that cycle.

When you hold Bitcoin, there's no counterparty. No bank to approve access. No institution that can debase what you own. It's yours — in full. Outside the reach of credit scores, bail-ins, or political games.

This is what true ownership looks like. With Bitcoin, you don't owe anyone anything. You're not "allowed" to use your wealth — you control it outright. No middlemen. No gate-keepers. No permission needed.

And unlike fiat, Bitcoin isn't fueled by debt. Its value comes from scarcity, not leverage. It doesn't need your enslavement to grow — it thrives on your exit.

Reflection Checkpoint

How much of your income goes to debt — not by choice, but by design?

What have you financed that you never truly owned?

Think about it — are you working for freedom, or for lenders?

If that question makes you uncomfortable, good. You're getting closer.

Bitcoin: The Exit Route from Debt

This control over your financial destiny is what makes Bitcoin so compelling. It offers a way out of the trap that traditional financial systems have laid for you — a chance to reclaim agency over your economic life. While banks profit from creating money out of nothing, Bitcoin's value is rooted in transparency and immutability — qualities that resist manipulation and inflation.

We've been conditioned to view debt as a necessary part of modern life — a tool to achieve our dreams or climb the ladder. But behind that narrative is a trap that keeps us tethered to jobs we hate and lifestyles we can't sustain, always borrowing from our future just to survive today. Debt promises freedom, but more often delivers servitude — an endless cycle of earning and paying that leaves little room for real autonomy.

Bitcoin breaks that cycle. It gives you a way to store and grow wealth outside the channels controlled by banks, governments, or credit systems. Its value isn't based on your FICO score or your employer's trust in you. It exists independently of policy, permission, or politics.

This independence is what makes it powerful. Bitcoin doesn't rely on your compliance — it thrives on your freedom. It gives you an exit not just from financial dependency, but from the narrative that says you can't own anything unless it's borrowed first.

As you look ahead in this chaotic financial landscape, ask yourself: What do you truly own? What assets do you hold that aren't attached to a monthly payment, a credit score, or a third party's approval?

This is where Bitcoin shines. It's unconditional. No hidden fees, no fine print, no centralized authority who can change the rules mid-game. Just pure, verifiable ownership — backed by mathematics, not manipulation.

Every dollar borrowed is another step deeper into a system built to extract from you. But seeing the trap is the first step toward escape. You don't need to reject every tool of modern finance — just stop believing it was built for your benefit.

Choose differently. Step out of the loop. And realize that real financial freedom isn't found in approval — it's found in sovereignty.

The Hard Numbers: How Bitcoin Compares

Numbers don't lie — but narratives often do. Over the past decade, Bitcoin has outperformed nearly every traditional asset class, year after year.

Since its inception, Bitcoin has averaged annual returns of 50% to 100%. Even during so-called "quiet" years, Bitcoin regularly outperforms every major asset class. Its long-term annualized return leaves Wall Street benchmarks in the dust. What began as an obscure digital experiment is now a financial force that even institutions can't ignore.

Compare that to the S&P 500 — the mainstream's gold standard. Over the long run, it returns about 7–10% annually. Respectable, sure. But those gains are tied directly to the fiat system — and fiat quietly eats itself from within. Stocks are not immune to monetary policy, inflation, or debt-fueled bubbles. Their upside is limited by the system they rely on.

And speaking of inflation — the official numbers lie. As mentioned above, the Consumer Price Index (CPI) conveniently excludes rising costs in essentials like food, energy, housing, and education. While the government claims 2–4%, real families know the truth: inflation is more like 10–15%. Wages don't keep up. Fiat savings lose purchasing power each year.

Bitcoin doesn't suffer from that erosion. Its 21-million-coin limit is fixed — no printing, no bailouts, no dilution. Fiat bleeds you slowly. Bitcoin holds the line.

What about gold? It's been the go-to inflation hedge for centuries, but it's returned only 1–2% annually over the past decade. It sits in vaults, unused and increasingly irrelevant in a digital-first economy. Gold is heavy, hard to move, and costly to store. When its price rises, more of it gets mined— there's no fixed supply. Bitcoin, on the other hand, is border-less, instant, accessible to anyone with a smartphone—and its supply is hard-capped at 21 million. No matter how high the price goes, the amount of new Bitcoin being mined declines over time, eventually reaching zero.

Real estate? It's tangible, but slow. After factoring in taxes, maintenance, and inflation, real annual returns are often just 2–5%. And your property is tied to geography, politics, and local economies. Bitcoin, by contrast, is liquid 24/7, portable across borders, and immune to eviction or seizure (if stored properly).

But Bitcoin isn't just an investment — it's a paradigm shift. Its decentralized design challenges the entire premise of central-ized financial control. For those disillusioned by rigged systems, Bitcoin isn't just a vehicle for returns — it's a rejec-tion of those systems altogether.

This isn't about chasing gains. It's about alignment — matching your financial choices with your values. Bitcoin offers more than upside. It offers agency.

So, ask yourself: Are you content with traditional paths? With 10% returns while inflation takes 15%? Or are you ready to pursue something built for individuals — not institutions?

The numbers don't just show performance. They reveal a pattern: the old system extracts. Bitcoin empowers.

What you do next is up to you — but make no mistake: the window is still open. And for those paying attention, the math speaks louder than the marketing.

CHAPTER 2
WHAT IS F*CK YOU MONEY?

"It's like F You money."

— MICHAEL SAYLOR, THE POMP PODCAST
#598

Redefining Wealth and Freedom

You're sipping coffee on a quiet morning. Your phone buzzes—an invite for an early meeting, and beneath it, a headline: something about a new scandal, a market panic, or the latest political distraction designed to keep you anxious or outraged. You glance at it, but you don't take the bait. You look outside instead. The world is buzzing, rushing, scrolling —but you don't have to. You could dive in. You could chase the calendar, join the hustle, stay plugged in. Or you could sit still.

That's the essence of F*ck You Money. It's not about piles of cash or flashy assets; it's about autonomy. True wealth isn't measured by how much you have, but by how little you need to ask permission. In a world built to bind you with golden chains, the real treasure is freedom—the power to say no without fear.

Traditional wealth often leads to dependence. Take property ownership—it's framed as the ultimate financial milestone, but comes with taxes, regulations, and obligations. You're not just buying a home; you're buying into a system that never stops demanding. Stocks, too, are tied to centralized platforms where your access can be restricted with a click. These assets may look empowering, but they're often just gilded cages.

It's time to shift the paradigm—from accumulation to sovereignty. Real freedom starts with financial independence. If your assets can be frozen, they're not truly yours. If they rely on third-party trust, it's not real liberty. Self-sovereignty means control without permission. It's not just a strategy—it's a mindset—one where you stop building your life around institutional approval and start designing it around personal autonomy.

Bitcoin embodies this shift better than anything else. It's portable, permissionless, and borderless. You can carry your wealth anywhere without restriction. Unlike traditional money tied to governments or institutions, Bitcoin transcends borders and defies censorship. You can transact freely—no gatekeepers, no approval needed.

Sound money leads to sound life planning. Bitcoin's fixed supply offers scarcity by design, making it a strong store of value in a world where most assets erode under inflation. Imagine holding something that doesn't decay—an asset rooted in code, not politics. It runs on the most secure computing network in human history—protected by global energy, verified by math, and immune to corruption. It's a foundation for anyone seeking stability, independence, and control in uncertain times.

Reflection Exercise

Take a moment to define what *wealth* means to you. Is it a number on a bank statement—or the ability to live life on your terms, free from financial constraint? Jot down your thoughts. How does freedom factor into your idea of success? Clarifying your definition will help you make better financial decisions moving forward.

Bitcoin redefines ownership at its core. Traditional assets come with strings attached—custodians, regulations, counterparty risk. But with Bitcoin, there's no intermediary, no approval process, no one to stop you. If you hold your private keys, your Bitcoin is truly yours. It can't be seized, censored, or frozen. It's not just ownership—it's sovereignty.

This is more than theory. Bitcoin eliminates counterparty risk by removing the need to trust anyone at all. You don't need a bank's permission. You don't rely on a company to stay solvent. You don't depend on a government to respect your rights. Bitcoin is a direct connection between you and your wealth.

You could travel anywhere in the world with your savings in your head, secured by your passphrase: no forms to fill out, no border restrictions, no exchange rates. Your wealth goes with you—uncensored, uninterrupted, unstoppable.

While traditional investments require trust in fragile institutions, Bitcoin relies only on math and code. It's governed by rules, not rulers. It doesn't care about your citizenship, your credit score, or your politics. It's a system built to resist corruption and protect your autonomy.

F*ck You Money isn't about hoarding wealth. It's about reclaiming your right to choose—your time, your work, your path. It's about aligning your financial life with your values in a world that wants you compliant and distracted.

So, consider what these ideas mean to you. Maybe it's a shift toward more independent assets. Perhaps it's a mindset change —one that stops waiting for permission and starts acting with conviction. However you begin, what matters is that you begin.

This book is your invitation to redefine wealth on your terms —not as accumulation, but as autonomy.

Why You've Been Trained to Depend on the System

Think back to school. Remember the endless drills, the memorization, the emphasis on rules over reasoning? You may have picked up some useful skills, but the deeper lesson was obedience. Schools didn't teach you how money works. They didn't teach you how to build wealth. Financial literacy wasn't forgotten—it was *excluded*. You were trained to fit into the system, not question it. Independence was never the goal. Compliance was.

Then came the workplace. You set out to climb the ladder, hoping for freedom at the top. But each step up tightens the grip. More responsibility means more pressure, not more autonomy. The "golden handcuffs" are real—they shimmer with prestige but bind you in time, stress, and obligation. A six-figure salary is nice... until it owns your calendar and your peace of mind.

Meanwhile, the financial industry profits from your confusion. Complexity isn't accidental—it's the business model. The harder it is to understand your options, the easier it is for middlemen to charge hidden fees and skim value from your work. Advisors benefit from your inertia. Cookie-cutter portfolios line their pockets, not yours. This isn't a broken system —it's a profitable one, working exactly as designed.

Bitcoin rejects this design. It has no CEO, no sales team, no glossy brochure. It spreads through discovery, not persuasion. It wasn't built to serve institutions—it was built to *escape* them. Bitcoin is a grassroots movement, born from frustration, sustained by education, and powered by people who refuse to be chained to systems that don't serve them.

Bitcoin doesn't ask you to trust—it asks you to *verify*. It doesn't require permission, credentials, or bank accounts. You don't need to convince anyone. You just need to learn. You can explore it on your own terms, at your own pace, and become your own bank when you're ready.

Imagine planning your future without worrying about frozen accounts or hidden policies. No middlemen. No approval process. No one to tell you what you can or can't do with your money. Bitcoin offers something radically simple: direct ownership.

When you hold your keys, you don't just own Bitcoin—you own your future. Nobody can seize it. Nobody can censor it. Nobody can dilute it. That kind of certainty is rare in a world of shifting rules and broken promises.

This isn't about rebellion for rebellion's sake—it's about choosing clarity over confusion, freedom over friction, and resilience over reliance.

Ask yourself: how much of your life is dictated by systems you didn't choose? What would change if your financial life were rooted entirely in something you control?

This chapter challenges you to rethink everything you've been taught about money, career, and control. The old model promised security but delivered dependence. Bitcoin offers a new model that demands more responsibility but returns *sovereignty*.

This isn't theory. It's happening. People are stepping off the treadmill and reclaiming their power—one block at a time.

The Psychology of F*ck You Money

What would it feel like to wake up and know nothing—and no one—owns your time? That your decisions aren't dictated by money, fear, or obligation? That's what F*ck You Money really represents. It's not about stacking cash just to brag—it's about autonomy. It's the confidence to walk away from anything that no longer serves you. It's wealth measured not in dollars, but in freedom.

This mindset doesn't begin with a bank balance. It starts with a mental shift. Everything changes when you stop seeing money as a finish line and start seeing it as a tool. Bitcoiners get this. They don't panic during downturns because they aren't playing the same game. Volatility doesn't scare them—it reinforces their conviction. They know the system is rigged, and they've opted out.

Bitcoiners don't seek permission. They don't ask financial advisors what to do. They've realized the most valuable thing you can own is conviction. Their calm isn't naivety—it's clarity. They understand that Bitcoin can't be printed into worthlessness, frozen by bureaucrats, or manipulated by suits in boardrooms. That kind of certainty changes how you see risk. It changes how you see the world.

Once you have true financial control, fear fades. You don't stress over market swings or job loss. You don't worry about whether a bank will approve your choices. You begin to think long-term. You gain peace, not because the world is calm—but because you are.

Bitcoin becomes more than an investment—it becomes practice for life. It demands self-responsibility. It forces you to slow down and think for yourself. And in doing so, it trains you to become sovereign—not just financially, but personally.

This shift touches everything. You stop asking, "Can I afford this?" and start asking, "Does this align with my values?" You stop chasing status and start seeking meaning. You stop reacting and start creating. That is real wealth: the ability to design your life from the inside out.

And something strange happens—you begin attracting others who live this way. The mask comes off. You no longer need to pretend, impress, or conform. You speak freely, live intentionally, and connect more deeply. You become dangerous to a system that thrives on passivity.

This transformation doesn't end with your portfolio. Once you've tasted freedom, you start questioning everything—how you work, who you trust, what you believe. You begin to see that much of what you were taught was designed to keep you small, dependent, and obedient. That clarity invites you to live differently.

Bitcoin is your gateway. It's not just digital money—it's a new lens. It doesn't promise safety; it promises responsibility. And in exchange, it gives you something priceless: power over your life.

This journey won't be easy. It asks you to question deeply and act boldly. But if you take it seriously, it will reward you with more than financial upside—it will reward you with clarity, peace, and purpose.

So, ask yourself: Where are you still playing small? Where are you waiting for permission? And what would it look like to stop?

F*ck You Money is the mindset of someone who's done waiting. Done obeying. Done pretending.

You don't have to be rich to start thinking this way.

But if you keep thinking this way, you might just end up free.

Why Bitcoin Is the Only True F*ck You Money

In 1933, President Franklin D. Roosevelt signed Executive Order 6102, forcing Americans to hand over their gold to the Federal Reserve. It was a clear message: your property is yours —until it isn't. Today, that risk remains. Banks can freeze your accounts without warning. Governments can seize assets in times of crisis. Bureaucrats you've never met can dictate your financial fate.

Bitcoin changes that. It's the first truly unconfiscatable asset. There's no issuer. No headquarters. No CEO. Just code, math, and your private keys. When you hold Bitcoin, no one can take it from you. No bank can lock you out. No official can cancel your access. You—and only you—control your money.

This isn't just security. It's sovereignty. Bitcoin can move without permission. It crosses borders without paperwork, banks, or delays. It doesn't rely on the goodwill of governments or financial institutions. It exists because the network exists—and because you choose to participate.

Bitcoin is the first form of true private property in the digital age. There's no counterparty risk. No brokerage. No custodian. Just you and your keys. That's what makes Bitcoin unique: its design protects you from seizure, censorship, and systemic failure.

Governments with ballooning debts will be tempted to seize private wealth. That temptation grows as the system strains. But Bitcoin resists this by design. Its decentralization makes it immune to single points of failure. It doesn't care who's in charge. It doesn't bend to pressure. It answers to no one.

This redefines the game. With Bitcoin, you're not just preserving wealth—you're rejecting coercion. You're opting out of systems that punish dissent and reward compliance. You're building a future on your terms.

Have you ever felt powerless when a bank denied you access to your funds? Or anxious about whether your savings could vanish in a crisis? That fear is built into the fiat system. Bitcoin removes it. It replaces trust in institutions with trust in code.

Bitcoin isn't just software—it's a philosophy. It's about decentralization over control, transparency over manipulation, and empowerment over dependence. It offers a way out—and a way forward.

This isn't just about leaving behind one system. It's about choosing a better one. One where people—not institutions—set the terms.

As you move into the next chapter and begin exploring how to integrate Bitcoin into your life, ask yourself: Are you ready to stop asking for permission? Are you prepared to take ownership of your financial future?

Bitcoin is your opportunity to do precisely that.

CHAPTER 3
BITCOIN IS DIFFERENT

"The further a society drifts from the truth, the more it will hate those who speak it."

— GEORGE ORWELL

Why Bitcoin Is Not Crypto

Picture a carnival—bright lights, loud music, and endless attractions promising excitement and novelty. But as you look closer, the illusions blur together. Many booths offer the same tricks in slightly different costumes. That's the state of the crypto market today: a noisy parade of altcoins, each claiming to reinvent money, yet most replicating the very fiat models they pretend to replace.

Bitcoin isn't one more booth at the carnival. It's the bulldozer clearing the entire fairground.

Bitcoin's birth was unlike anything else in finance. It wasn't launched with a press release or funded by venture capitalists.

There was no pre-sale, no insider allocation. In 2009, an anonymous figure named Satoshi Nakamoto released Bitcoin into the world with open-source code, available for anyone to use or ignore. No marketing campaign. No centralized control. Just a quiet revolution seeded in public.

That launch matters. It means Bitcoin didn't start as a way to make a quick buck. It started as a way to opt out of a rigged system. In contrast, most altcoins launch with pre-mined tokens and insider deals. They replicate Wall Street's games under the guise of decentralization—early access, gatekeeping, profit extraction. Their structures mirror the very inequality they claim to oppose.

Then there's Bitcoin's code: hard-coded rules with no exceptions. No bailouts, no new supply, no hidden inflation. There will only ever be 21 million coins—ever. That's monetary policy enforced by math, not committees. Altcoins? Many change their rules at will, like companies updating terms of service. What's decentralized today may be rug-pulled tomorrow.

Bitcoin is not just rare—it's reliable. Most altcoins live and die on hype cycles, inflated by promises and deflated by reality. They act more like casino tokens than money. Volatile. Fragile. Designed for speculation. Bitcoin, in contrast, is a system built for permanence. It doesn't rely on trends. It's indifferent to price action. It was engineered to survive chaos.

And that's why Bitcoin isn't just another crypto asset—it's the sovereign layer of a new financial reality. Others may come and go with flashier branding or slicker tech. But Bitcoin is the bedrock. It is the foundation on which the future will be built, and it cannot be replaced.

If Bitcoin isn't just another crypto token, then what is it really? To understand its value, you have to stop thinking like a trader—and start thinking like someone who owns something *scarce*. Bitcoin isn't just a tech play. It behaves more like digital property—and that changes everything.

Bitcoin Is Digital Gold—But Stronger

Bitcoin is often called *digital gold*, and for good reason. Like gold, it's scarce, durable, and not controlled by any government. But unlike gold, it's far easier to store, transfer, and verify. You don't need a vault, a middleman, or a border crossing. You can send Bitcoin anywhere in the world in minutes —and audit the entire supply from your laptop.

Gold has long served as a store of value because of its physical properties. But Bitcoin's strength comes from its mathematical properties: provable scarcity, predictable issuance, and the inability to counterfeit or inflate it. That makes it even more secure as a foundation for long-term savings.

In short: Bitcoin takes what gold does well—and upgrades it for the digital age.

Bitcoin Is Better Than Real Estate

Bitcoin is often compared to digital gold—but in many ways, it also behaves like digital real estate.

You don't need a down payment. You don't need to qualify for a mortgage. You don't need to take on debt, hire a property manager, or fix a leaky roof. You can buy your digital property one brick at a time, with whatever amount you're ready to invest—whether it's $10, $100, or $10,000. No middlemen. No waiting. No permission.

Like real estate, Bitcoin is scarce, valuable, and can be borrowed against without selling. But unlike property, it's instantly liquid, globally portable, and divisible down to the smallest unit. There are no property taxes. No zoning laws. And no geographic limitations.

That's why many see Bitcoin not just as an alternative to traditional assets—but as an *upgrade*.

> *"They're reluctant to buy Bitcoin and they tell me, 'You can't live in a Bitcoin.' That is precisely why you want to have Bitcoin as the asset that collateralizes the entire financial system. The very fact that you can't live in it means you can demonetize the thing you can live in—and make that much cheaper relative to this."*
>
> — PETER DUNWORTH

Reflection Exercise

Consider your motivations for exploring cryptocurrency. Are you seeking quick gains or long-term security? Reflect on how Bitcoin's principles align with your financial goals—and how they differ from the promises of altcoins. Write down your thoughts and revisit them as you continue your journey through this emerging financial landscape.

You've just seen how Bitcoin mirrors and improves on the best aspects of gold and real estate. Now, envision it as the bedrock of a new economic order—a digital gold standard that transcends borders and political agendas. Its decentralized nature ensures that no single entity can control or manipulate the network, making it an ideal medium for true financial sovereignty. While other cryptocurrencies may offer flashy features or niche applications, they often lack Bitcoin's resilience and foundational strength.

The allure of Bitcoin lies not in hype or speculation but in its power to redefine how we think about money. It challenges the status quo by decentralizing control and empowering individuals to take ownership of their financial future—free from the failures and corruption of intermediaries.

As you dig deeper, remember that Bitcoin is more than just software—it is a philosophy rooted in transparency, accountability, and self-determination. It offers a clear path toward reclaiming control over your economic life while challenging outdated ideas of wealth and power.

Choosing Bitcoin over altcoins—or over any form of centralized money—isn't just an investment decision. It's a statement of values: a commitment to sustainability over hype, and integrity over opportunism. It's a step toward building a world where financial independence is truly accessible—not just for insiders or early movers, but for anyone willing to opt in.

Let this reflection guide your decisions as you explore this evolving landscape. Are you aligning with systems of control or ones of empowerment? Are you chasing trends—or building something lasting?

This chapter invites you to move beyond accumulation and toward autonomy. To step into a future shaped not by speculation, but by conviction. A life of intention. A journey rooted in integrity, transparency, resilience, connection, freedom, and truth.

How Bitcoin Actually Works (Without Tech Overload)

Bitcoin runs without a boss, a bank, or a boardroom. No single entity makes the rules. Instead, it operates on a decentralized network of computers called nodes. These nodes verify and agree on every transaction using a consensus mechanism—an honest, methodical process where thousands of participants keep each other in check. This decentralized model ensures no one can cheat, censor, or quietly change the system to benefit themselves.

Miners are the network's frontline defenders. They dedicate computing power to secure the system by solving complex mathematical problems. Roughly every ten minutes, a miner adds a new "block" of verified transactions to the blockchain. This process, known as mining, isn't just for show—it ensures that Bitcoin is scarce and tamper-proof. And every four years, the network cuts the mining reward in half, slowing the creation of new coins and reinforcing long-term scarcity.

Every transaction ever made is recorded publicly on the blockchain. It's a permanent, unchangeable ledger that anyone can audit. At the same time, your personal identity stays private. This radical transparency ensures the system remains honest, while protecting individuals from intrusion or surveillance. Once a transaction is confirmed, it becomes part of an incorruptible digital history.

Bitcoin was designed to get stronger under pressure. It's antifragile—built to evolve and harden after every attack or attempted exploit. Just as the internet improved through decades of stress and resistance, Bitcoin adapts with each challenge. It doesn't just survive; it learns and improves.

That evolution doesn't come from a central authority or committee. Bitcoin upgrades only happen when there's broad consensus across its global network of users, miners, and developers. Improvements are proposed, debated publicly, and adopted voluntarily—if at all. This process is deliberately slow, and that's a feature, not a flaw. It ensures that core principles like scarcity and decentralization remain intact, even as the network strengthens over time.

What makes Bitcoin radically different from the financial systems we're used to is that it cannot be changed on a whim. Its monetary policy is locked in. The total supply is capped at 21 million coins—forever. No central bank can "stimulate" the Bitcoin economy by printing more. This gives Bitcoin a rare feature in modern finance: predictability.

It's also open to anyone. Bitcoin doesn't care who you are, where you live, or what paperwork you have. You don't need a bank account. You don't need permission. All you need is an internet connection. This breaks down barriers for the billions excluded by traditional financial systems. It's money that says yes when institutions say no.

Another cornerstone is its resistance to censorship. With traditional banks, your account can be frozen, your transactions blocked. Bitcoin works differently. Once you send it, it flows through the network until it's confirmed—unstoppable. No third party can halt or reverse it. That's not a bug—it's a feature.

Bitcoin is trustless by design. You don't need to rely on a third party to hold your assets or verify your balance. You hold your keys. You control your funds. There's no banker or broker standing between you and your money.

This isn't just a better payment system—it's a shift in how value is stored and exchanged. Bitcoin is a protocol, not a product. Like the wheel or the internet, it solves a deep-rooted problem: how to transfer value without trusting middlemen. It's engineered money for a digital world.

And it's not going away. Unlike hyped-up crypto projects or tech startups chasing exit strategies, Bitcoin is built to endure. It's slow to change, deliberately so. Because strength comes from consistency, not trend-chasing.

Right now, Bitcoin is still in its early stages. Adoption is growing, but it's not yet saturated. That won't last forever. Those who understand it today are ahead of the curve. And that curve is steep.

Bitcoin moves forward whether you're ready or not. As the system grows and strengthens, the cost of not understanding it grows with it.

Bitcoin isn't just money—it's a declaration of independence from a rigged system. It puts power where it belongs: in your hands.

Bitcoin Is Engineered for Freedom

Bitcoin doesn't beg for permission. It doesn't care who you are, where you're from, or whether your government thinks you're worthy of owning wealth. Its supply is locked at 21 million—no bailouts, no backdoors, no inflation "stimulus" to dilute your savings. Unlike fiat currencies that crumble under political pressure, Bitcoin remains untouched. It's monetary truth in a world built on economic lies.

You don't need a bank account. No ID. No gatekeeper. Just access to the internet. That's the power of open finance— where anyone, anywhere, can participate without asking for approval. While traditional finance excludes the poor and undocumented, Bitcoin says, *you're in.*

No one can stop your transaction. No one can freeze your account. Once your Bitcoin is on-chain, it's unstoppable— flowing like water through censorship. Try freezing that.

And unlike fragile fiat systems built on trust in institutions that betray it, Bitcoin doesn't ask for trust. It's trustless by design. You hold the keys. Literally. No third-party needed, no counterparty risk. Just you, your wallet, and your sovereignty.

These principles echo the Austrian school of economics, which long warned against fiat currencies, central banking, and the erosion of individual sovereignty through inflation. Thinkers like Ludwig von Mises and Friedrich Hayek argued that real freedom requires sound money—money the state can't manipulate. Bitcoin puts their ideas into action. It removes the power to print from corrupt institutions and returns it to math, code, and individuals. Many Bitcoiners arrive here after discovering Austrian economics. Others find Austrian thought because they found Bitcoin first. Either way, the alignment is undeniable: decentralization, scarcity, and voluntary exchange—no rulers, no bailouts, no theft by inflation.

People in collapsing economies already live this truth. When banks shut down and paper money becomes worthless, Bitcoin keeps working. It's not a theory. It's survival. And it's already saving lives.

Even without a bank account, you can get Bitcoin. Around the world, people are buying it with cash at ATMs, trading peer-to-peer, or earning it directly through mobile apps. In places where traditional banking fails, Bitcoin meets people where they are—with just a phone and a few sats, they're in the system.

Bitcoin's rules aren't up for debate. No insider can rewrite the protocol. No government can "stimulate" away its value. It's a solid foundation in a world of shifting sands—a fortress built for the digital age.

And this isn't just about technology—it's about empower-ment. In a world that thrives on dependency, Bitcoin lets you walk away. It puts you in control of your economic future, your wealth, and your choices.

As adoption accelerates, the chance to accumulate large amounts may shrink—but the real opportunity isn't about quantity. Bitcoin is engineered to protect and grow purchasing power over time. Even modest exposure has historically outperformed inflation, gold, real estate, and the stock market. Whether you join early or late, the destination is the same: sovereignty, security, and freedom from a broken system. Nothing stops this train. Jump on at any stop—you're still getting out of fiat.

Bitcoin isn't just engineered for freedom. It's built for people like you to finally live it.

This Is Not a Trend — This Is the New Base Layer

Fire changed how we eat. The wheel changed how we move. Bitcoin changes how we own. It's not just another tech tool—it's a foundational invention, the first incorruptible form of money in a world built on economic manipulation. This isn't hype. It's infrastructure for a future that demands something better than fiat games and gatekept finance.

Bitcoin was born for the internet age. While legacy financial systems stumble through bureaucracy and exclusion, Bitcoin flows seamlessly across borders, permissionless and open to all. Banks demand paperwork. Bitcoin demands nothing. It doesn't care who you are. It just works—globally, 24/7, without middlemen.

This isn't a passing trend. Apps come and go. Coins pump and dump. Bitcoin endures. It's not here to chase hype—it's here to outlast it. Its design resists fragility. Its purpose rejects centralization. Bitcoin isn't trying to be the next thing. It's trying to be the *last* thing—the base layer for everything that comes next.

Adoption moves fast. The early internet felt like a curiosity—until it reshaped the world. Bitcoin is doing the same. We're in the frenzy stage now—the Bitcoin gold rush. It's never too late to join, but the early days won't last forever. The longer you wait, the harder it is to be early. Each cycle pulls more people in. Each time, it gets harder to ignore. This is your moment, before the institutions arrive and pretend they invented it.

Bitcoin doesn't wait. It doesn't slow down for regulators, headlines, or hesitation. It accelerates as the world catches on —offering an exit from broken systems that serve the few and trap the rest. If you've ever felt let down by traditional finance, this is your invitation to opt out.

Banks protect themselves first. Governments inflate your savings away. Bitcoin flips that script. It puts power in the hands of the people—borderless, decentralized, and incorruptible. It's a tool for the excluded. A lifeline for the locked out. A weapon against financial coercion.

Bitcoin is internet-native money for a borderless age. It breaks through bureaucracy like code breaks through censorship. No gatekeepers. No delays. Just a direct connection between you and your economic freedom.

This is your chance to build on something permanent. Not just to survive the system—but to transcend it. Bitcoin isn't just a currency—it's a movement. One built on transparency, accountability, and individual empowerment.

As we close this chapter, think about where you stand. Are you following legacy systems down a familiar dead end—or stepping into a new financial frontier where *you* set the rules?

Bitcoin is not a trend. It's the new base layer.

CHAPTER 4
HOW TO GET STARTED

Buying Bitcoin Without Getting Burned

Getting started with Bitcoin doesn't have to be complicated—but the first step is critical. Choosing a reliable exchange sets the tone for your entire experience. Don't gamble with shady platforms that charge high fees or have a history of mismanagement. Stick with trusted, Bitcoin-focused onramps like Swan or Cash App. These platforms prioritize simplicity, transparency, and security, helping you get started without unnecessary risk.

Before buying, you'll likely encounter something called Know Your Customer (KYC). These are identity verification rules designed to prevent fraud and money laundering. While KYC can make the process feel more official, it's not without trade-offs. You're handing over personal data that could be compromised if the platform is ever breached. It's a balance between convenience and privacy—and you should make that trade knowingly, with an understanding of the risks. While there are non-KYC options out there, many of them come with limited support or higher chances of being targeted by scammers.

Speaking of scams—this space is full of them. Be extremely cautious. Ignore random DMs, giveaway promises, or influencers claiming they'll double your Bitcoin. That's textbook fraud. If it sounds too good to be true, it is. The best defense is skepticism. Trust is earned slowly in Bitcoin, not offered freely to strangers on the internet.

A smart way to begin your journey is with dollar-cost averaging (DCA). This means buying small, consistent amounts of Bitcoin on a set schedule—daily, weekly, or monthly. It removes emotion from the equation. No more stressing about timing the market or catching the perfect dip. Over time, this strategy helps you build a strong position while ignoring the noise of day-to-day price swings. It's about stacking slowly and staying focused on the long term.

One thing to expect—because it happens to almost everyone: as soon as you buy, the price will probably dip. It's like Bitcoin knows. Don't panic. This is normal. Sometimes it takes days, weeks, or even months for your buy to feel "right" on the chart—but that's not the point. DCA helps you ignore those moments. You're not trying to win a trade—you're building a long-term position in the strongest asset on earth. Stack, zoom out, and keep going.

Just one rule: never buy more than you can afford to lose in the short term. Bitcoin is volatile, and there will be sharp drops. Only commit what you won't need to pull out if things get rocky. That's how you hold with conviction—and sleep at night.

Reflection Exercise

Take a moment to reflect on your financial goals and how they align with your approach to Bitcoin. Consider setting aside a monthly budget for dollar-cost averaging and committing to it for six months. Write down your thoughts on how this strategy might alleviate stress and build confidence in your investment plan.

It's essential to understand that the journey into Bitcoin isn't about instant gratification—it's about playing the long game and building real wealth over time. Patience and persistence are your allies. Focus on *time in the market*, not attempts to time the market. This mindset shift can be liberating, freeing you from the anxiety of daily chart-checking and allowing you to enjoy life's simple pleasures without financial worry.

As you embark on this journey, remember that Bitcoin represents more than just an investment; it's a new way of thinking about money and personal independence. It challenges conventional wisdom and offers an alternative path toward financial sovereignty. By equipping yourself with knowledge and using caution when choosing platforms and strategies, you position yourself for long-term success.

This chapter has aimed to empower you with practical insights—how to navigate exchanges, understand KYC, avoid scams, and apply strategies like dollar-cost averaging. With these fundamentals in place, you're better prepared to take control of your financial future.

In the rapidly evolving world of digital finance, knowledge is power—a compass guiding you toward financial freedom. Embrace this challenge with confidence, knowing you're not alone in the pursuit of autonomy within a system designed to empower rather than control.

Whether you're driven by curiosity, frustration with the status quo, or a desire for change, this journey offers more than potential gains. It's an opportunity for personal growth, intentional living, and redefining what wealth truly means—on your own terms.

Where to Keep It — Wallets 101

> *"There is only one way out. And one way to ensure your freedom. And that's Bitcoin in self-custody. Bitcoin in self-custody is digital 1776."*
>
> — RUSTIN, *SIMPLY BITCOIN*

So, you've got some Bitcoin in your digital pocket. Now what? It's crucial to understand where your Bitcoin actually resides. Spoiler: it's not floating in the cloud or stored on a server somewhere. The keys to your kingdom lie in your wallet—and choosing the right one can make all the difference.

Think of a custodial wallet like a bank vault where someone else holds the keys. You're trusting them not to lose, freeze, or misuse your Bitcoin. But as the saying goes: not your keys, not your coins. You're ultimately relying on someone else's integrity—and history has shown how risky that can be.

On the other hand, a non-custodial wallet puts those keys directly in your hands. You become the true owner, with no middlemen. It's the essence of sovereignty—no strings attached. But with that power comes responsibility: if you lose your keys, there's no one to call. Your Bitcoin could be gone forever. So, this choice isn't just technical—it's foundational. It determines who controls your assets: you, or someone else.

If you're just getting started, mobile wallets offer a beginner-friendly path to self-custody. Apps like *Muun*, *Phoenix*, and *BlueWallet* are easy to use and great for small amounts and everyday transactions. They're like carrying cash in your pocket—quick, accessible, and practical. But they're not ideal for storing larger amounts long-term, as they're still connected to your phone and the internet.

For long-term security, hardware wallets are the gold standard. Devices like *Trezor*, *Ledger*, and *Coldcard* act like digital safes—keeping your private keys offline, protected from hackers and software vulnerabilities. They're built for serious savers who want to hold for the long haul. While there's an upfront cost and a learning curve, the tradeoff is peace of mind and serious protection for your assets.

If you want a balance between independence and backup support, collaborative custody offers a compelling middle ground. This setup uses multisig wallets—where multiple keys are required to move your Bitcoin. Services like *Unchained Capital* and *Casa* let you hold one key while they securely hold the others. It's a great option for inheritance planning or managing larger holdings, because no single point of failure can lock you out. You retain control, with a safety net.

Case Study: Choosing the Right Wallet

Meet Anthony, a newcomer eager to dive into Bitcoin but wary of potential pitfalls. After researching options, he starts with a mobile wallet for its convenience and ease of use. As confidence grows and holdings increase, he decides to invest in a Trezor hardware wallet for added security. Recognizing the importance of legacy planning, he explores collaborative custody with Unchained Capital for larger reserves. This layered approach balances accessibility with security, reflecting Anthony's evolving needs as a Bitcoin holder.

Each wallet type serves its unique purpose, catering to different user preferences and situations. Mobile wallets provide flexibility for everyday transactions; hardware wallets offer fortress-like protection for larger reserves; collaborative custody ensures continuity and disaster recovery. By understanding these distinctions and their implications for control and security, you're better equipped to choose the wallet that aligns with your goals and risk tolerance.

This isn't just about securing Bitcoin; it's about securing peace of mind. It's about empowering yourself with choices that reflect your values and long-term goals within the digital economy. Whether you're just starting out or looking to optimize existing strategies, these insights help you make informed decisions that prioritize both convenience and security without compromising either.

As you navigate these choices, remember: the key lies in understanding where your Bitcoin truly lives—within your private keys. These keys are the foundation of ownership and autonomy in this decentralized world. By using mobile wallets for daily spending, hardware wallets for savings, or collaborative custody for long-term planning, you keep control where it belongs—with you.

Choose what fits your needs today, but stay flexible. Your circumstances will evolve, and so should your setup. That's the essence of Bitcoin self-sovereignty: empowering yourself to adapt, protect, and thrive on your own terms.

Mistakes Newbies Always Make

Picture this: you're sitting at your desk, eyes glued to a screen filled with charts that dance and flicker, each tick a heartbeat. The allure of trading is strong, promising quick gains and the thrill of the chase. But beneath this excitement lies a trap that's snared many a newcomer. Most traders, despite their best intentions, end up on the losing side. The market's volatility is not a game of chance but a test of patience. Timing the market often backfires because it's less about predicting the next move and more about weathering the storm. Volatility, while intimidating, rewards those who wait. Instead of trying to outsmart the market, understand that patience is your ally. Let others chase the highs and lows; your focus should remain steadfast on the bigger picture.

The crypto world is noisy, filled with distractions that can easily lead you astray. Altcoins, with their promises of exponential returns and revolutionary tech, beckon like sirens. But remember, Bitcoin is the signal amidst this cacophony. Everything else is noise that dilutes your focus, pulling you away from the core thesis. Altcoin hype can be intoxicating, yet it often leads to diluted portfolios and empty promises. It's easy to get caught up in the frenzy of the next big thing, but this can distract from Bitcoin's steady progress and long-term potential. Stick to what you know holds value—Bitcoin's resilience and foundational strength. Avoid getting sidetracked by every new coin that claims to change the world.

Leaving your coins on an exchange might seem convenient, but it's akin to leaving your valuables out in the open, hoping they'll be safe. The collapse of platforms like FTX, Celsius, and BlockFi serves as poignant reminders of what can go wrong when trust is misplaced. These institutions can fail spectacularly, sometimes overnight, taking your assets down with them. "Not your keys, not your coins" is a fundamental truth. By entrusting your Bitcoin to an exchange, you relinquish control over your assets. It's crucial to understand that exchanges are not invincible; they're vulnerable to hacks, mismanagement, and regulatory pressures that can jeopardize your holdings.

One of the most common pitfalls is selling too soon. The temptation to cash out at the first sign of profit is strong, especially when faced with market fluctuations that test your resolve. But selling early is a form of self-sabotage that can cost you dearly in the long run. Not only do you incur taxes on realized gains, but you also risk missing out on Bitcoin's potential upside. This isn't a sprint; it's a marathon. The real game lies in long-term conviction and understanding that Bitcoin's value proposition extends well beyond short-term price movements. Selling prematurely often stems from fear or a lack of understanding about Bitcoin's true potential.

In this landscape, overconfidence is a double-edged sword. The minute you believe you've mastered the market is when it humbles you. It's easy to get swept up in moments of success, but the market has a way of teaching humility through losses that can wipe out gains in an instant. Confidence should be rooted in knowledge and tempered by awareness of risks. Rather than viewing yourself as an expert after a few wins, approach every decision with caution and informed insight. Remember that even seasoned investors continue learning and adapting.

The path to Bitcoin success isn't paved with shortcuts or get-rich-quick schemes; it requires diligence and discipline. Avoid the trap of thinking you can beat the market at its own game without understanding its intricacies. Accept that learning is an ongoing process and that mistakes are part of growth. Each misstep offers lessons that refine your strategy and strengthen your resolve.

As you navigate this world, keep in mind that Bitcoin represents more than mere financial gain—it embodies a shift in how we approach wealth and independence. It challenges traditional systems by offering an alternative built on transparency and decentralization. Embrace its nuances while recognizing that true mastery comes from continuous exploration rather than momentary triumphs.

The path to Bitcoin success isn't paved with shortcuts or get-rich-quick schemes; it requires diligence and discipline. Avoid the trap of thinking you can beat the market at its own game without understanding its intricacies. Accept that learning is an ongoing process and that mistakes are part of growth. Each misstep offers lessons that refine your strategy and strengthen your resolve.

As you navigate this world, remember that Bitcoin represents more than financial gain—it represents a shift in how we approach money, independence, and long-term thinking. It challenges the traditional system by offering an alternative rooted in transparency, decentralization, and personal responsibility. True mastery doesn't come from a lucky trade or viral tip—it comes from patient exploration and conviction built on experience.

By reflecting on the pitfalls shared here—trading traps, altcoin distractions, exchange vulnerabilities, and premature selling—you equip yourself to move forward with clarity and confidence. The journey doesn't end with avoiding mistakes. It deepens as you continue learning, questioning, and aligning your actions with your values.

This isn't just a financial shift—it's a mindset shift. One where freedom, patience, and understanding guide your decisions, and where success is measured not just in gains, but in growth.

Building Real Conviction

In the fast-paced world of Bitcoin, it's easy to get caught up in daily price swings. Each uptick can feel like victory; each dip, a crisis. But this short-term mindset often obscures the bigger picture. To truly appreciate Bitcoin's potential, you have to zoom out.

Bitcoin is best understood not by watching every tick of the chart but by stepping back—like viewing a complex painting from a distance. What looks like chaos up close becomes a coherent vision when seen in full. The same is true with Bitcoin's historical price cycles, which reveal a consistent pattern of growth, resilience, and recovery. What feels like volatility is energy—a frequency vibrating through markets, shaking out weak hands, and signaling the arrival of something new. Bitcoin is volatile not because it's unstable, but because it's alive. It's vibrating its way to infinity.

This broader view helps build confidence. It shows that Bitcoin isn't just surviving—it's evolving through volatility. The key is perspective. By focusing less on short-term noise and more on long-term trends, you develop the clarity and conviction needed to stay the course.

Insights from Thought Leaders

Learning from the right sources is a crucial part of building strong conviction. Look to those who have spent years studying and advocating for Bitcoin—people like Michael Saylor, who explains its value with clarity and depth; James Seyffart, who brings a data-driven perspective; and Robert

Breedlove, who explores its philosophical implications. These voices offer more than opinions—they provide frameworks that help you understand Bitcoin's role in a changing economic world.

In contrast, the noise from hype-driven influencers can derail your progress. TikTok personalities and social media promoters often dangle promises of quick riches but rarely offer substance. Their excitement may be loud, but it's rarely lasting. Focus instead on educators who value accuracy over buzz, and who treat Bitcoin as a long-term movement—not a passing trend.

Long-Term Perspective

Understanding the difference between high and low time preference is key to building conviction. Bitcoin naturally promotes a low time preference—a mindset that values patience, saving, and long-term thinking over instant gratification. It's not about chasing short-term wins; it's about planning for the future.

Think of it like planting a seed. With consistent care and patience, it grows into something strong and lasting. That's the approach Bitcoin encourages: steady, disciplined action over decades, not days. This mindset is the opposite of gambling, which hinges on quick gains and emotional decisions. Bitcoin invites you to slow down, zoom out, and prioritize the long-term well-being of both yourself and future generations.

Diligent Inquisition

A strong Bitcoin conviction isn't built on blind belief—it's forged through curiosity, research, and a refusal to take things at face value. In a space flooded with hype and misinformation, separating signal from noise requires ongoing vigilance.

Question everything. Cross-check sources. Stay skeptical— even of this book. Use it as a launchpad, not a final destination. The more perspectives you explore, the clearer your understanding becomes. Prioritize facts over feelings, and look for insights backed by evidence, not emotion or marketing spin.

By cultivating a habit of critical thinking, you strengthen your foundation. This discipline not only builds lasting conviction, it prepares you to navigate Bitcoin's complexity with clarity and confidence.

The Resilience of Conviction

Real conviction isn't about blind belief—it's about building a foundation rooted in understanding. When you've taken the time to study Bitcoin's history, learn from credible voices, and embrace a long-term mindset, you become far less vulnerable to fear, doubt, and market noise.

This kind of conviction transforms how you think about wealth, responsibility, and independence. It's not just about holding an asset—it's about reshaping your relationship with money in a way that aligns with deeper values.

Let this chapter serve as a reminder: conviction comes from knowledge, not hype. It's a steady force that helps you stay grounded, especially when others are panicking or distracted. When you truly understand what Bitcoin is and why it matters, you're equipped to make better decisions—not just financially, but philosophically.

Next, we'll explore how Bitcoin is already influencing the world beyond individual portfolios—how it intersects with social movements, economic systems, and cultural narratives. With your conviction in place, you're ready to see Bitcoin not just as an investment, but as a tool for broader transformation.

CHAPTER 5

THE WEALTH STRATEGY

"You don't have to do anything. Just buy it and wait. The hardest thing is to do nothing."

— MICHAEL SAYLOR

The Power of Hodling

In the chaos of fast-moving markets, where traders chase every tick and news alert, a different approach stands in quiet contrast: HODL. Born from a typo in a 2013 Bitcointalk forum post — where a user meant to type *hold* but wrote HODL — the term quickly became a cultural rallying cry: "Hold On for Dear Life." What began as an accident evolved into a philosophy grounded in patience, conviction, and long-term thinking.

Hodling isn't just a strategy—it's a rejection of short-termism. Traders often believe they can outsmart the market, but most end up underperforming a simple buy-and-hold approach.

The allure of timing the market is strong, but the reality is humbling. Volatility punishes overconfidence, while time rewards discipline.

Early Bitcoin adopters who held through extreme highs and brutal crashes weren't just lucky—they were committed. Even those who bought during peaks like the 2017 bull run and stayed through the downturn were ultimately rewarded when Bitcoin surpassed $60,000 in later years. These stories reflect more than profit—they reflect belief in Bitcoin's long-term value.

Hodling is also a mindset of sovereignty. In a world that promotes immediate gratification and constant action, choosing to hold is an act of resistance. It's about aligning with Bitcoin's deeper ethos: decentralization, independence, and the power to opt out of a system built on instability. Hodlers aren't ignoring volatility—they're choosing to rise above it, trading noise for clarity and short-term wins for lasting freedom.

Reflection Exercise

Take a moment to consider your investing journey. Have there been times when hype or fear pushed you into a rushed decision? What might have happened if you'd paused instead—if you had chosen patience? Write down a few of those moments. This reflection can help you better understand your tendencies and reinforce the long-term thinking that defines a strong hodl mindset.

Embracing hodling is a bit like practicing mindfulness. It teaches you to stay grounded, focusing on what matters instead of getting lost in distractions. In the same way mindfulness helps you stay present, hodling helps you stay aligned with your values—choosing long-term growth over short-term gratification.

Bitcoin challenges the traditional financial model, which thrives on noise, urgency, and constant movement. Instead of scrambling to buy and sell, hodling encourages you to build something durable—based on scarcity, transparency, and decentralization. This shift allows you to rethink what wealth means and how it's built.

For many, this isn't just a financial breakthrough—it's an emotional one. Hodling removes the pressure to react constantly, creating space for more important parts of life. You don't need to track charts 24/7. You can spend your time and energy on the people and passions that matter most.

This approach doesn't mean ignoring reality. It means choosing how to respond to it. Volatility becomes a challenge to grow through, not something to fear. In the process, you build a strategy—and a mindset—that can carry you through financial ups and downs with clarity and confidence.

There's no single path to financial independence, but hodling offers a solid starting point. It's a practice of discipline and resilience, rooted in long-term vision rather than short-term wins. It reminds us that real wealth isn't just about numbers —it's about freedom, stability, and having the time and space to live on your own terms.

Time in the Market Beats Timing the Market

Trying to predict the highs and lows of the market is a trap many fall into, yet few succeed. Most who attempt to time the market end up frustrated or worse—broke. Dollar-cost averaging offers a simpler, more effective alternative. By committing to buy a fixed amount of Bitcoin at regular intervals, you remove emotion from the equation. You buy more when the price is low, less when it's high, and over time, you build a meaningful position without stress or second-guessing.

Compare the lives of day traders with long-term holders. Traders constantly watch charts, reacting to every movement and riding an emotional rollercoaster. Wins are short-lived; losses can be devastating. Meanwhile, many long-term holders see the best gains when they stop obsessing over the price. Often, life gets busy, they step away, and they come back wealthier. Volatility punishes impatience and rewards discipline.

DCA transforms investing into a habit. Like brushing your teeth or going to the gym, it becomes part of your routine. That consistency builds conviction over time. You stop chasing headlines and start focusing on goals. Slowly, your stack grows—and with it, your confidence in Bitcoin's potential.

This strategy aligns with low time preference: the mindset of delaying gratification in exchange for greater rewards later. In a culture obsessed with immediacy, developing this outlook is powerful. Building wealth through Bitcoin is like planting a tree—it takes time, care, and patience, but the payoff is generational.

High time preference leads to impulsive decisions and short-term thinking. Low time preference encourages thoughtful planning, long-term perspective, and the ability to withstand volatility. It's not about perfection—it's about showing up consistently and trusting the process.

Take two investors: Jaimie tries to buy low and sell high, jumping in and out of the market. Ashley sticks to a monthly DCA plan. Years later, Ashley's strategy outperforms Jaimie's, not because Ashley was smarter, but because she was more consistent. No stress, no trading—just disciplined, steady accumulation.

The strength of DCA lies in its simplicity. There's no need to study charts or follow market influencers. You just invest regularly and let time do the heavy lifting. Over the long haul, this strategy has proven more successful than most attempts to beat the market.

If you've felt overwhelmed by volatility or exhausted by indecision, DCA can bring clarity and peace of mind. It's a strategy rooted in discipline and trust—not in trends or hype. With each purchase, you take another step toward financial sovereignty.

Ultimately, this is about more than just building wealth. It's about aligning your actions with your long-term goals, values, and vision for the future. In a world full of noise and distraction, dollar-cost averaging offers a clear path forward.

Remember: time in the market beats timing the market. Every single time.

Why "Never Sell" Makes Sense

One of the most powerful strategies for long-term wealth with Bitcoin is adopting a "never sell" mindset. Rather than cashing out and severing your future upside, consider borrowing against your Bitcoin when liquidity is needed. This approach preserves your position while allowing you to access cash for expenses, investments, or life events—without triggering capital gains taxes or sacrificing long-term growth.

Instead of viewing retirement as the moment to liquidate, imagine entering it without selling a single satoshi, the smallest unit of Bitcoin. By borrowing against your Bitcoin, you tap into your wealth without realizing taxable events. Your holdings continue to compound while you use the borrowed funds as needed, maintaining exposure to Bitcoin's potential over the decades to come.

Platforms like Unchained and Ledn offer collaborative custody lending models that prioritize both security and autonomy. These services allow you to retain partial control over your Bitcoin while leveraging it as collateral, reducing risks tied to centralized platforms. This model aligns with Bitcoin's core principles—sovereignty, transparency, and decentralization—while offering practical financial tools in the modern age.

Think of your Bitcoin as the foundation for a legacy. Selling may provide temporary relief, but holding and borrowing can preserve generational wealth. Passing on your Bitcoin without converting it to fiat means handing down a durable store of value, giving future generations a financial advantage free from inflation and systemic risk.

Each time you resist the urge to sell, you preserve your asset's potential to appreciate. Selling short-circuits growth. Borrowing, on the other hand, allows your Bitcoin to keep working for you while giving you access to liquidity when you need it. It's a long-term approach that protects your principal and aligns with the goal of sustainable, compounding wealth.

> *"We live in a system that must grow exponentially — or collapse."*
>
> — JEFF BOOTH

Traditional finance often pushes liquidation as the default path to liquidity. Bitcoin flips that script. It gives you the option to retain ownership while still meeting financial needs. Instead of constantly trading in and out, you build stability and flexibility over time, strengthening your financial position against uncertainty.

In this new paradigm, Bitcoin is more than an investment—it's a strategic asset that can fuel your financial goals without the compromises of fiat thinking. Borrowing against it reflects trust in the long-term thesis and enables you to maintain control, even as life evolves.

This strategy isn't about never accessing your wealth—it's about accessing it intelligently. When you shift from a sell mindset to a borrow-and-hold approach, you redefine wealth on your terms. You create space for autonomy, resilience, and legacy.

True wealth isn't just what you accumulate—it's what endures and empowers across generations. By aligning your financial plan around "never sell" principles, you invest in more than Bitcoin's price—you invest in a philosophy of long-term strength, control, and sovereignty.

Your Exit Plan Is No Exit

Bitcoin isn't just a temporary refuge from the broken financial system—it's the endgame. As fiat currencies lose relevance, the idea of "cashing out" becomes less appealing. Why would you exit into a system you've deliberately chosen to opt out of? Bitcoin offers something deeper: a new financial paradigm rooted in freedom, scarcity, and transparency. It's not about fleeing a flawed structure—it's about arriving at one that finally works.

In this vision, Bitcoin becomes the foundation of everyday life. You buy coffee, invest in startups, or purchase real estate —directly in Bitcoin. Thanks to innovations like the Lightning Network, transactions are nearly instant and virtually free. What once seemed futuristic—buying a home with sats or securing a renovation loan without touching fiat—is increasingly within reach. More people are moving in this direction every day.

That said, spending Bitcoin directly still triggers capital gains taxes under current law, which complicates day-to-day use.

Every cup of coffee or online purchase becomes a taxable event. For this reason, borrowing against your Bitcoin is often the better strategy—it lets you access liquidity without triggering a sale, preserving your long-term upside and avoiding unnecessary tax consequences.

But getting there requires a mindset shift. Bitcoin must evolve in your life from an eccentric side bet to a central pillar of your wealth strategy. Save in Bitcoin. Build with Bitcoin. Borrow against it when needed. A growing ecosystem of Bitcoin-native services—secure lending platforms, business tools, payment rails—is making this vision more practical than ever. Aligning with this movement puts you on the side of resilience, innovation, and long-term thinking.

> *"A lot of you have a Mercedes, or a 401(k), and you don't have a Bitcoin. The price is only $86K—it's on sale. Don't come back in 20 years telling me I have what you should've had. You have exactly what you deserve, and so do I. Fix your life. Buy your Bitcoin."*
>
> — AMERICAN HODL (EDITED FOR CLARITY
> AND LANGUAGE)

Fast-forward 30 years. What legacy will you leave? A fading 401(k)? Or an incorruptible asset that's still gaining value, secured by math and immune to the whims of central banks? Bitcoin offers the opportunity to pass on not just wealth, but sovereignty—a foundation your family can build on for generations.

This is about more than numbers. It's about living in a world where your wealth isn't tied to manipulated interest rates or government bailouts. Bitcoin is decentralized, apolitical, and global. It offers a hedge against inflation, a shield from financial surveillance, and a path toward authentic security.

And in that context, the whole idea of "exiting" Bitcoin starts to sound backwards. Why plan to leave something that offers more freedom and opportunity than what you'd be exiting into? Instead, go deeper. Contribute. Educate. Innovate. Build. The more you engage with Bitcoin's development and community, the more you help shape its future.

This shift—from short-term gains to long-term sovereignty—transforms how you approach money. It encourages you to think generationally. To dream bigger. To imagine entire industries rebuilt on decentralized infrastructure. It's a radical redefinition of wealth—based not on how fast you can flip assets, but on how deeply you can build value that lasts.

Bitcoin is more than an investment. It's a way to reclaim control. A way to reject broken systems and help build something better. When you stop thinking about your "exit" and start thinking about your role in what's coming, the real journey begins.

As a small thank-you, I'd like to share a resource that's been invaluable to me: Swan Bitcoin, the platform I trust for all my Bitcoin purchases.

Swan is designed to help you build long-term wealth with Bitcoin through simple, automated savings plans. It's perfect for new investors, focusing on education and simplicity with tools and resources to help you understand Bitcoin's potential as revolutionary digital money.

With Swan, you can set up recurring purchases—a strategy called dollar-cost averaging—to steadily grow your Bitcoin holdings without the stress of market timing. The platform also stands out for its low fees, robust security, and exceptional customer support, making it an ideal choice for anyone starting their Bitcoin journey.

Sign up with this link and get $10 in Bitcoin for free: swanbit coin.com/naloisio

Thank you for your generosity and support.

Your fellow hodler,
Nick Aloisio

CHAPTER 6
THE GREATEST WEALTH
TRANSFER IN HISTORY

"If wars can be started by lies, peace can be started by truth."

— JULIAN ASSANGE

The Ticking Clock

B itcoin, with its cap of 21 million coins, represents a monetary system like no other. Unlike fiat currencies, which can be printed at will and devalued through political manipulation, Bitcoin's supply is hard-coded—immutable and transparent. Not even its creator can alter the rules. This digital scarcity forms the foundation of its value and sets it apart from every currency that came before.

Roughly every four years, the Bitcoin network experiences a halving. This event cuts the reward for mining new Bitcoin in half, reducing the number of new coins entering circulation. Each halving amplifies scarcity, and historically, it's also triggered sharp increases in price. The simple truth: when supply tightens and demand grows, price tends to follow.

Bitcoin joins the ranks of transformative innovations—alongside the printing press, electricity, and the internet—as a technology that reshapes how we live, connect, and transact. It's ushering money into the digital age, offering a decentralized alternative to systems that many believe no longer serve them. Just as the internet disrupted communication, Bitcoin is disrupting finance.

And with that disruption comes a shrinking window of early opportunity.

Adoption is accelerating. Institutions are entering. Awareness is spreading. If you're reading this now, you're still ahead of the curve—but the gap is closing. As more people understand Bitcoin's role as a hedge against inflation and a tool for long-term wealth preservation, the chance to front-run that demand diminishes.

We're following a familiar pattern: slow beginnings, then exponential adoption. Think of the internet in the early '90s —barely noticed, often misunderstood. Then it changed the world. Bitcoin's adoption curve mirrors other technological S-curves, where steady early growth is followed by rapid acceleration.

Why does this matter? Because timing and conviction matter. Waiting on the sidelines while demand continues to rise may cost you the most powerful advantage available right now— being early. Getting in before the crowd means more than a better entry price. It means influence, leverage, and the ability to build while others are still waking up to what's happening.

Reflection Exercise: Timing Your Entry

- **Assess Your Financial Position:** Where does Bitcoin fit in your current strategy? What portion of your portfolio are you comfortable allocating?
- **Understand Your Risk Tolerance:** How well do you handle uncertainty? Bitcoin is volatile, but so is being unprepared.
- **Set Clear Goals:** Are you investing for growth, preservation, or financial sovereignty? Bitcoin supports all three, but your goal shapes your approach.
- **Choose Your Entry Method:** Will you buy a lump sum or use dollar-cost averaging? Establish milestones to review progress and adjust as needed.

This chapter is about more than capitalizing on price action. It's about choosing to participate in a deeper shift—one that redistributes financial power away from centralized institutions and into the hands of individuals. Bitcoin is not just an asset; it's a signal. A vote. A tool for reclaiming agency in a system that often thrives on your dependence.

Those who grasp this now are positioning themselves not just for potential financial upside—but for alignment with a global movement. One that values transparency over manipulation, freedom over permission, and sovereignty over servitude.

The decisions you make today matter. Not just for your portfolio, but for your future autonomy. Bitcoin isn't a get-rich-quick scheme. It's a get-free-slowly tool. The opportunity is here, but won't always be this good.

Make your move.

The Institutional and Nation-State Space Race

Imagine a chessboard stretching across the global economy. Every move sends ripples through markets, institutions, and nations. In this new game, Strategy made one of the boldest opening moves. Led by Michael Saylor, the company didn't just buy Bitcoin—it redefined what a modern corporate balance sheet could look like. Saylor's strategy was simple but powerful: "Don't sell your Bitcoin, sell debt." Instead of treating Bitcoin as a side bet or hedge, he made it the foundation. And rather than sell it to raise money, he borrowed against it—turning Bitcoin into a strategic reserve asset that could generate liquidity without giving up future upside.

At the nation-state level, El Salvador shocked the world by becoming the first country to adopt Bitcoin as legal tender. It wasn't just symbolic—it was a bold bet on financial independence. The country started mining Bitcoin with volcanic energy, issued Bitcoin bonds, and invited the world to pay attention. Some mocked them. Others watched closely. But no one could ignore it. El Salvador wasn't just experimenting—it was leading.

Now institutions are rushing in. BlackRock, Fidelity, and other legacy giants are entering the space with Bitcoin spot

ETFs—funds that hold actual Bitcoin, unlike earlier futures-based ETFs that only tracked contracts and often underperformed. It's not curiosity—it's necessity. They know what's coming. If they miss this moment, they risk becoming irrelevant in a financial system that's shifting underneath them. These companies aren't just dipping a toe—they're building bridges between the old world of finance and the new one powered by digital assets.

What we're seeing now isn't just an arms race—it's a space race. One country or institution makes a move, and others are forced to respond or risk being left behind. The first-mover advantage is real. Nobody wants to be the last to adopt a technology that could define the next century of finance. Game theory is at play here: once the race begins, staying out becomes riskier than joining in.

Bitcoin is no longer just a speculative asset. It's a strategic play. For institutions, it's about staying competitive. For countries, it's about sovereignty and survival. And for you, it's about understanding where the world is going—and getting there before everyone else does.

This global race is still in its early stages, but it's picking up speed. With proposals like U.S. President Donald Trump's call for a strategic Bitcoin reserve and legislative moves like the Lummis-Gillibrand bill aiming to give Bitcoin clearer regulatory footing, the shift is becoming harder to ignore. As major players position themselves for the next era of finance, individuals have a rare chance to do the same. You don't need billions to benefit from this transformation. You just need conviction—and the ability to move before the herd.

What Strategy and El Salvador understood early on is now becoming mainstream. The opportunity to front-run this shift is shrinking. You still have time—but not forever. As adoption ramps up, so will demand. And the price will follow.

So, the question becomes: are you going to wait until this race is over—or are you going to claim your position while it's still early?

The Broken Fiat Machine Can't Keep Up

The global financial system is starting to look like a crumbling structure—creaking under the weight of endless debt and bad incentives. Governments around the world, in a desperate attempt to keep things afloat, are printing money at unprecedented levels. Dollars, euros, yen—it doesn't matter the name, the pattern is the same. The more they print, the more broken the system becomes. Debt is no longer the exception—it's the foundation. And future generations will be left holding the bill.

Inflation is the silent thief in all of this. Most people rely on official stats like the Consumer Price Index (CPI), but as I mentioned previously, those numbers are designed to look good. What matters isn't the headline number—it's how much less your money buys each year. As Michael Saylor put it, inflation is a vector: it has direction and force. And it's draining your purchasing power, even if you don't see it happening in real time.

This isn't theory—it's reality in places like Turkey and Argentina, where inflation has spun out of control and faith in national currencies has collapsed. People are waking up and looking for alternatives. Even in the U.S., confidence in the dollar is eroding. When people start to question their money, the cracks in the system become impossible to ignore. That's when Bitcoin enters the picture—not as a get-rich-quick scheme, but as a peaceful exit.

Bitcoin isn't just another asset. It's the upgrade the system needs. It's decentralized, transparent, neutral, and immune to manipulation. No central bank can dilute it. No politician can rewrite its rules. It's a financial foundation you can trust—one where the code is law and the rules don't change mid-game.

The fiat system has no real answer to Bitcoin. Reform efforts are just temporary patches—like trying to fix a sinking ship with duct tape. The problem isn't just mismanagement; it's the design itself. Fiat money is built on promises, trust, and control. Bitcoin is built on math, verification, and freedom.

As trust in traditional currencies continues to decline, Bitcoin offers a digital lifeboat—a way to protect your wealth from inflation, corruption, and policy failure. It gives individuals the power to secure their financial future without needing permission from anyone. In a world full of uncertainty, that kind of sovereignty is priceless.

This shift isn't about fear—it's about opportunity. It's about challenging the assumptions we've inherited about money, savings, and value. And it's about building something stronger in their place. When you choose Bitcoin, you're not just investing—you're opting out of a broken system and stepping into a better one.

Take a moment to reflect: Have you felt trapped by rising costs or disillusioned by financial promises that never materialize? Bitcoin doesn't claim to fix everything—but it offers a foundation that's stronger, fairer, and finally built to last.

Why You're Still Early — But Not for Long

It's easy to feel like you've already missed the boat. With headlines about Bitcoin ETFs, treasury companies like Strategy and Metaplanet posting exponential gains, Trump's Strategic Bitcoin Reserve, and price surges dominating the news again, you might wonder: *Am I too late?* But here's the reality—on a global scale, Bitcoin adoption is still under 5%. That means more than 95% of the world hasn't joined this movement yet. You're not late. You're early. The door is still open.

Think back to the early days of the internet or smartphones. At first, only the curious or the bold got involved. Most people stood on the sidelines, skeptical or unsure. Then slowly, almost imperceptibly, these tools became essential parts of life. Bitcoin is following that same path—only faster. At first, it feels slow, then suddenly it's everywhere. That's where we are right now: on the edge of exponential growth.

Taking action today puts you ahead of the crowd. By the time the masses catch on, the price will likely be much higher— not because Bitcoin's fundamentals changed overnight, but because demand outpaced supply. This is what early adoption looks like: you get the front-row seat while everyone else is still standing in line.

And here's the good news: you don't need to be wealthy to participate. You just need the willingness to act before the herd does. Start small if you have to. The key is starting. This moment is still early—but it won't be forever.

Bitcoin's value isn't just in price. It's in what it represents: financial freedom, self-sovereignty, and a break from systems built to keep you dependent. Choosing Bitcoin is more than just an investment—it's a statement. A declaration that you want something better. Something fairer. Something you can trust.

Being early takes courage. It means seeing the potential before it becomes obvious to everyone else. But that's also where the greatest opportunities live. As we head into the next chapter, we'll explore how Bitcoin is influencing broader social and economic change. For now, just remember this: you're not behind—you're exactly where you need to be.

CHAPTER 7
BITCOIN CHANGES YOU

"The most important skill for getting rich is becoming a clear thinker — who doesn't care what others think."

— NAVAL RAVIKANT

Bitcoin and Low Time Preference

Time preference is about how we value now versus later —how much we're willing to delay gratification for something better down the road. A high time preference leans toward spending today and dealing with the consequences later. A low time preference means thinking long-term, planning, and resisting short-term temptations. In a fiat-based world, everything is designed to push you toward the former. Easy credit, low interest rates, and constant advertising all work together to keep people consuming, not saving.

Bitcoin shifts that. It rewards patience. Instead of nudging you to spend, it encourages you to hold, plan, and build. It pulls your attention toward the future—toward goals that might take years to achieve, but are worth waiting for. This isn't just a financial change. It's a mindset shift. You start making different choices—not because someone told you to, but because your priorities change.

There's a popular phrase in the Bitcoin community: "You don't change Bitcoin. Bitcoin changes you." That's exactly what happens. The protocol doesn't adjust to market whims or emotional reactions. It requires discipline. It rewards consistency. And over time, it helps you build that same steadiness in your life. Saving becomes a form of empowerment. You stop chasing trends and start acting with intention.

This shift affects more than just money. It changes how you think. You start asking, "Does this expense move me toward my goals?" "Is this worth the time it took to earn it?" You become more mindful. Each satoshi saved feels like progress—like you're opting out of a broken system and choosing something better.

Reflection Exercise

Take a moment to reflect on your spending habits over the past month. Jot down three purchases that brought fleeting joy but no lasting value. Now consider three investments in yourself—whether in skills, experiences, or savings—that align with your long-term goals. Reflect on how each has impacted your sense of purpose and direction.

As this mindset shift deepens, you'll find yourself stepping away from the endless consumerism pushed by fiat culture.

You become more than just a buyer of things—you become a builder of value. Your energy moves from acquiring to creating. That might mean launching a project, learning a new skill, or simply laying the foundation for a legacy that lasts. Bitcoin empowers this shift. It puts the focus on ownership—of your time, your resources, and your future.

That transformation spreads to other parts of your life. Relationships get stronger when you stop chasing distractions and start prioritizing meaning. You begin to favor shared experiences over status symbols. You become more intentional with your time—because time, like Bitcoin, is scarce and worth protecting.

In this new framework, money is more than currency. It becomes a moral compass. You start to see how wealth, when handled with integrity, can be used as a force for good. You begin to align with a growing global movement—one that values transparency over manipulation, and personal empowerment over dependency.

Bitcoin's protocol enforces scarcity, but paradoxically, it also reveals abundance. It clears away the noise of consumer culture and offers a path where freedom is measured not by what you own, but by how you live.

As you adopt this low time preference mindset, remember: real wealth isn't just about accumulation. It's about fulfillment. About living deliberately and building a life aligned with your values—not the ones handed down by a broken system, but the ones you choose for yourself.

Bitcoin invites you to pause and ask what truly matters. Are your habits shaped by conviction or by conditioning? Are your choices building the life you actually want?

That's the real power here—not just financial resilience, but inner strength rooted in clarity, purpose, and self-sovereignty.

Bitcoin and Responsibility

Holding Bitcoin means holding responsibility. There's no customer support to call, no password reset if you lose access to your keys. It's up to you—and that's exactly the point. Bitcoin hands you the reins and says: You're in charge now. For some, that can feel intimidating. But for many, it's the most empowering shift they've ever experienced. When you hold your own keys, you're not just storing value—you're stepping into full ownership of your financial future.

That kind of ownership is almost unheard of in the fiat world. Banks and payment processors control your access. They can freeze your account, deny a transaction, or delay your money for "review." In a fiat system, you don't own your wealth— you lease it. Bitcoin flips that script. It puts you in full control. There's no middleman, no gatekeeper. You're not being managed—you're managing.

This shift from dependency to sovereignty changes how you see everything. It's not just about holding Bitcoin—it's about rejecting systems built on blind trust. In the fiat world, you're expected to believe that governments won't debase your currency and that banks will act in your best interest. But with Bitcoin, the rule is simple: *verify, don't trust*. The code is open. The ledger is public. You don't need to believe—you can check for yourself. That's what makes Bitcoin different. It replaces blind faith with radical transparency.

Taking responsibility for your wealth builds resilience. Every time you make a conscious choice—whether it's learning how to self-custody, moving funds, or securing your keys—you're becoming stronger. You're building habits that carry over into every part of your life. Confidence grows. Independence deepens. You stop relying on others to solve your problems, because now you know you can solve them yourself.

This kind of strength isn't just financial—it's personal. It shows up in how you make decisions, how you handle setbacks, and how you face uncertainty. You don't need someone else's approval. You don't need a safety net held by fragile institutions. You've built your own.

And yes, mistakes will happen. You might fumble a wallet setup, misplace a seed phrase, or make a poor decision along the way. That's part of it. But with every stumble, you learn. You adapt. You level up. Owning Bitcoin is also about owning your outcomes—for better or worse. That's what real maturity looks like.

This path leads to something bigger than financial security. It's about becoming a steward of your own purpose. You start to live with more intention. You hold yourself accountable. You develop the discipline to think long-term and act with conviction.

Bitcoin doesn't just challenge the financial system—it challenges us. It forces us to rethink what it means to be responsible in a digital age. Not dependent. Not deferential. Responsible. And with that responsibility comes freedom.

So, take it seriously. Don't wait for someone else to manage your life. The old systems weren't built for your benefit—and they never will be. Bitcoin gives you an alternative. A way to break free, reclaim your autonomy, and live on your own terms.

That's not just a financial revolution—it's a personal one.

Bitcoin and Mental Clarity

Bitcoin offers something increasingly rare in today's financial world: clarity. For many who adopt it, this clarity becomes more than just economic—it becomes psychological. The stress of constantly watching market trends, reacting to every economic headline, or second-guessing financial decisions starts to fall away. There's no need to chase short-term gains or obsess over every fluctuation. Instead, you begin to embrace long-term conviction.

This shift is more than tactical; it's liberating. Your financial life becomes simpler. One asset, one mission. Bitcoin narrows the focus and reduces the noise. You stop trying to keep up with every move in traditional markets, and you start focusing on what really matters to you. Freed from constant speculation, your attention shifts to areas where you can actually grow—creatively, professionally, personally.

Conviction begins to replace confusion. Instead of constantly wondering whether you've made the right investment decision or hedging between multiple options, you find peace in principle-based decision-making. You stop checking the price and start checking in with your values. You align your actions with a long-term vision that's grounded in integrity and clarity. This discipline doesn't just impact your portfolio; it spills over into your daily life.

As financial anxiety fades, intention takes its place. You're no longer reactive—you're deliberate. Financial discipline evolves into life discipline. You spend with purpose, invest with care, and measure success in fulfillment rather than accumulation. What once felt like a constant battle for control now becomes a smooth and steady progression toward a future you believe in.

This clarity changes how you navigate complexity. Decisions are no longer made out of fear or social pressure. They come from a grounded sense of direction. You begin to recognize which commitments enhance your life and which distract from it. You set boundaries more easily. You prioritize better. You become more effective—not by hustling harder, but by tuning into what truly matters.

Mental clarity builds emotional resilience. When setbacks arise, they don't shake you. You face uncertainty with a sense of preparedness rather than panic. You learn to adapt with composure, to evolve instead of collapse. This mindset fosters growth—not just survival. You start to view adversity as a teacher, not a threat.

With financial pressure reduced, you begin to design a more balanced life. Health becomes a higher priority. Relationships take deeper root. Experiences take the place of possessions. You start valuing quality over quantity in everything—from how you spend your time to who you spend it with. You attract others who share your values, creating stronger connections and a shared sense of purpose.

This transformation reaches far beyond finance. As your choices align with your beliefs, your life begins to reflect your truest self. You resist societal definitions of success and build your own instead—grounded in authenticity and personal fulfillment. You no longer chase trends; you set your course with intention.

Bitcoin serves as an anchor in a chaotic world. Its reliability allows you to take risks elsewhere—in your creative pursuits, your career goals, your relationships—without the fear of financial ruin. That security fuels innovation. It frees you to dream bigger, to build boldly, and to move confidently.

What begins as a financial decision eventually becomes a personal awakening. You release the baggage of outdated thinking. You let go of scarcity mindsets and short-term fears. You embrace new ways of being that support your evolution.

Of course, this isn't an easy road. The journey toward clarity requires self-honesty. It asks you to confront distractions, bad habits, and inherited beliefs. But the payoff is immense: a more peaceful mind, a more intentional life, and a deeper sense of meaning.

In the end, wealth isn't just about what you hold in your wallet—it's about what you carry in your heart. Bitcoin may start as an investment, but it becomes a filter for everything. A tool to help you declutter, refocus, and live in alignment with what matters most.

Bitcoin as a Spiritual Shift

Bitcoin has become more than just a financial asset—it's a lens through which people are rethinking life itself. For many, stacking sats isn't simply a savings strategy; it's a ritual. Each satoshi saved is a quiet act of rebellion, a commitment to integrity, sovereignty, and purpose. This isn't just about wealth accumulation. It's about living in alignment with values that truly matter.

What makes Bitcoin so radical is its honesty. It cannot be manipulated, inflated, or corrupted by central authorities. Its open ledger is built on transparency. When you anchor your financial life in something incorruptible, it influences how you think, how you act, and how you relate to others. Bitcoin rewards clarity, truth, and discipline—and those principles begin to shape your mindset far beyond your wallet.

This spiritual dimension of Bitcoin often begins with frustration—frustration with fiat systems, with broken incentives, with a world built on debt and deceit. But from that disillusionment comes hope. Bitcoin offers an alternative. It brings together people from all over the world who are seeking something better. Not just better returns, but a better foundation for how to live.

The global Bitcoin community feels like a digital tribe—united not by borders, but by beliefs. Decentralization. Self-sovereignty. Personal responsibility. These are more than buzzwords. They form a code of ethics—a shared language built on memes, open-source contributions, and hard-earned lessons. The result is a culture where ideals like freedom, truth, and empowerment are celebrated and defended.

In this culture, money is no longer just a means to an end. It becomes a moral compass. Your spending reflects your principles. Your savings reflect your priorities. You begin asking harder questions: Does my financial behavior align with my purpose? Am I living with intention, or just consuming by habit? This kind of introspection isn't just financial—it's spiritual.

Bitcoin prompts us to reevaluate the stories we've been told about success. It's not about how much you own, but how honestly you live. True prosperity isn't measured in digits, but in how deeply you're connected to your values, your community, and your mission. In this new worldview, wealth is redefined. It's not about hoarding—it's about helping. It's not about power—it's about freedom.

This transformation also invites humility. You begin to see yourself as part of something larger. The Bitcoin protocol doesn't care about your status or your ego. It treats everyone equally. In that neutrality, there's a kind of grace—a reminder that fairness is possible when systems are designed to be incorruptible.

As Bitcoin shifts your relationship with money, it often shifts your relationship with yourself. You become more curious, more intentional, more reflective. You start to see growth not as an external race but as an internal evolution. You invest in learning, health, creativity, and relationships—things that compound in ways fiat never could.

Ask yourself: Has Bitcoin changed your priorities? Do you find yourself less interested in flashy purchases and more interested in meaningful work? Are you building things that last, rather than chasing short-term dopamine hits? These shifts matter. They reflect a deeper awakening.

Bitcoin invites us to step into integrity—not just with our finances, but with our entire lives. It offers a path to wholeness, where what you believe, what you value, and how you act are all in sync. This is the essence of spiritual alignment: living in truth, even when the world around you is built on illusion.

And that's the real gift. Bitcoin doesn't just change how we save—it changes how we see. It wakes us up. It pulls back the curtain on systems designed to exploit, and it hands us the tools to build something better—not just economically, but personally, relationally, even spiritually.

This chapter marks the culmination of Bitcoin's transformative power. What begins as a financial revolution becomes a revolution of the soul. You find yourself choosing growth over stagnation, clarity over confusion, sovereignty over submission. You begin to live with conviction.

So, the next time you save in sats, pause for a moment. Feel the intention behind the act. Understand that you're not just stacking digital coins—you're aligning with a deeper truth. You're opting out of a broken system and opting into a life of purpose.

This is the shift. And it's just beginning.

CHAPTER 8
A NEW SYSTEM IS ALREADY EMERGING

"You never change things by fighting the existing reality. To change something, build a new model that makes the existing model obsolete."

— BUCKMINSTER FULLER

The Rise of Parallel Economies

B itcoin communities around the world are quietly building new economies outside the legacy system. These grassroots networks operate on peer-to-peer trade and value-for-value exchanges, using Bitcoin not just as a currency, but as a tool for autonomy and resilience. They're creating local economic loops that prioritize trust, self-reliance, and freedom from centralized control.

One of the most visible examples is Bitcoin Beach in El Salvador. What began as a small initiative has transformed the local economy, enabling residents to pay for groceries, medical care, and utility bills with Bitcoin. Fiat currency is no longer essential in this town. The model has sparked a global movement, inspiring similar projects in communities eager to reclaim financial power from institutions that have historically failed them.

Meetups and conferences have become critical hubs for this transformation. These aren't just networking events—they're launching pads for real-world collaboration. As Bitcoin circulates within local ecosystems, wealth stays in the community instead of being siphoned off by distant intermediaries. These circular economies grow stronger as participants support one another directly, without relying on banks or corporate platforms.

Opting out of the fiat system builds more than financial freedom—it builds local strength. Small farms, family-run services, and freelancers are integrating Bitcoin into their businesses, skipping over red tape and embracing borderless, censorship-resistant commerce. This keeps value within the network and reinforces shared purpose.

And while institutions move slowly, individuals don't have to. Acting now—before Bitcoin adoption becomes mainstream— offers a strategic advantage. You can experiment with new financial models while others wait for permission. This early adoption mindset positions you ahead of the curve.

Bitcoin isn't just a new financial tool—it's a movement. Change doesn't need to come from governments or corporations. You don't need to lobby for reform or wait for approval. You can start building something better today, alongside others who share your values.

What sets this movement apart is its accessibility. Anyone can join. No credentials or connections are required. Bitcoin's decentralized nature removes gatekeepers, offering a way in for those shut out of traditional systems. As more people opt in, they contribute to a growing network that values fairness and freedom over profit and control.

The rise of parallel economies isn't just about escaping fiat—it's about creating alternatives that reflect who we are and what we care about. You're not just stepping out of the old system—you're stepping into something more human, more connected, and more resilient.

Reflection Exercise

How could you bring these principles into your own life? Start by asking: Are there local Bitcoin meetups or circular economy projects you can support—or even start? Could you begin integrating Bitcoin into your daily transactions, side hustle, or business operations?

These actions aren't just financial moves—they're steps toward resilience, independence, and community empowerment. Whether it's paying a freelancer in sats, joining a local Bitcoin group, or simply supporting businesses that accept it, each choice helps strengthen the parallel economy.

This sub-chapter explored how communities around the world are building economic loops outside of traditional systems—using Bitcoin to trade, collaborate, and create wealth that stays local. These grassroots efforts thrive without waiting for approval from institutions. They're bottom-up systems grounded in fairness, autonomy, and shared values.

As you reflect, consider where you can step into this momentum. Supporting or participating in Bitcoin-based communities is more than opting out of fiat—it's opting into a future built on connection, purpose, and freedom.

You have a role to play. What will it be?

Bitcoin and the End of Financial Surveillance

Your bank account is suddenly frozen. Your credit card declines without warning. You call customer service, only to hear that your funds are on hold due to "suspicious activity." No details, no appeal—just a digital wall between you and your money. It happens more often than you think. In the fiat world, control and censorship are built-in features, not bugs. The credit cards and banks we rely on operate behind a curtain of rules we never consented to. Every transaction is tracked, every anomaly flagged. Donations get blocked. Accounts are blacklisted. Your financial life becomes a reality show you never signed up for—scored, judged, and surveilled.

Bitcoin flips this dynamic on its head. By design, it resists censorship. Transactions are unstoppable and permissionless. There's no CEO to pressure, no headquarters to shut down, no off-switch to flip. Its integrity is preserved by a decentralized network where every participant reinforces the system. That means you can send Bitcoin to anyone, anywhere, at any time—no forms to fill out, no gatekeeper to please. It's finance built on autonomy, not approval.

Real-world events highlight the need for this kind of freedom. In 2022, Canadian truckers protesting government mandates had their bank accounts frozen. Platforms like GoFundMe and PayPal blocked donations. Political contributions were flagged. These weren't isolated incidents—they were coordinated demonstrations of financial control, dressed up as public safety. When access to your own money becomes conditional, the urgency for alternatives becomes crystal clear.

But here's the key distinction: in every one of those incidents, Bitcoin itself wasn't the problem. The censorship occurred at the edges—on centralized exchanges and donation processors. The protocol remained untouched. Users who held their own keys had uninterrupted access to their funds. Those relying on custodians were at risk. This underscores a fundamental truth: when you self-custody your Bitcoin, you preserve your financial voice. You own it—completely and unconditionally.

Bitcoin protects basic rights by making privacy and autonomy more than ideals—they're baked into the protocol. In a world where surveillance capitalism is the default, that's nothing short of revolutionary. Opting into Bitcoin means stepping out of a system that monetizes your data and limits your freedom. It's about reclaiming ownership over your economic identity.

This isn't just a tech upgrade. It's an act of resistance. Choosing Bitcoin is a declaration that your financial decisions are yours alone—not subject to manipulation by faceless institutions or middlemen with hidden agendas. It's not paranoia—it's proactive protection. It's taking the steering wheel back from a system that prefers you in the passenger seat.

Bitcoin offers a kind of sanctuary—a space where transactions are free from coercion, profiling, or interference. Where your financial actions reflect your values, not the preferences of surveillance-based platforms. Aligning with Bitcoin isn't just about privacy—it's about dignity. It's about participating in an ecosystem that respects your agency and treats your choices with integrity.

This alignment also represents a deeper philosophical shift. It's a rejection of systems that exploit your personal data and your dependency for profit. Bitcoin replaces that dynamic with one rooted in transparency, openness, and mutual respect. You join a community of builders and protectors—people dedicated to preserving economic freedom through innovation and decentralized power.

As legacy systems double down on control, dressed as "security," ask yourself: who benefits? And what happens when dissent becomes inconvenient? Bitcoin offers an escape from that spiral—an opportunity to transact on your own terms, with peace of mind that your data, your wealth, and your voice can't be arbitrarily silenced.

True ownership means having assets that can't be seized with the flip of a switch. It means being able to support causes you believe in without fear of retribution. It means no longer depending on permissioned platforms to live your life. That's the kind of power Bitcoin enables—quiet, resilient, and untouchable.

This isn't just about rejecting the old—it's about redefining what's possible. A new paradigm is emerging: one built not on fear and restriction, but on empowerment and inclusion. Not on exclusion and compliance, but on freedom and self-direction.

And as we continue through this book, keep one truth close: financial autonomy isn't theoretical. It's real. It's available. And it begins the moment you decide to claim it.

Embracing the Freedom to Innovate

In the world of Bitcoin, innovation doesn't wait for permission. There are no gatekeepers deciding who gets to build or what ideas are worth funding. Bitcoin's decentralized ethos creates a wide-open arena where creativity can flourish—untethered from bureaucracies, corporate filters, and legacy approval systems. Here, the only requirement is vision and the willingness to act.

Builders in the Bitcoin space aren't just tweaking existing systems—they're reimagining them entirely. Armed with open-source tools and aligned by shared values, these creators bypass investor mandates and instead focus on utility, freedom, and user empowerment. They're not constrained by the need to chase ads or shareholder profits. Instead, they prioritize merit, integrity, and necessity.

This freedom is fueling transformation across sectors. In media, podcasts and platforms built around Bitcoin principles are emerging—funded directly by audiences through sats streaming and value-for-value exchanges. No middlemen, no algorithms prioritizing outrage, no censorship from ad buyers. Creators speak freely, and listeners reward content that resonates.

In education, new Bitcoin-inspired learning platforms are replacing standardized, top-down curricula with critical thinking, financial literacy, and economic sovereignty. These programs empower students not just to memorize—but to question, understand, and build.

The Lightning Network is accelerating innovation by making microtransactions instant and inexpensive, unlocking use cases that were previously impossible. From pay-per-second streaming to micro-grants for independent research or open-source software, value can now flow freely in small, friction-less increments—removing old economic barriers to creativity.

Healthcare and finance are beginning to feel the ripple effects too. New platforms are exploring ways to give patients full control over their data using Bitcoin-based identity and record systems. And in finance, services built on Bitcoin are reaching the unbanked—not through charity, but through self-sovereign infrastructure that anyone can access with a smartphone and a seed phrase.

What all of these innovations have in common is a deep respect for the individual. Bitcoin's framework doesn't just invite innovation—it demands it. It asks us to build things that serve real needs, protect user freedom, and operate with transparency.

We are only beginning to understand what's possible when innovation is untethered from institutions that once decided who got to speak, build, and thrive. In Bitcoin's world, anyone can contribute. Anyone can create. And that alone is revolutionary.

Revolutionizing Content Creation

In the emerging Bitcoin-powered creative economy, value-for-value models are turning traditional content monetization on its head. Instead of relying on platforms that extract a cut of every interaction, creators are now connecting directly with their audiences—no middlemen, no permission required. This shift enables a cleaner, more honest exchange: value flows straight from the listener, viewer, or reader to the person creating the work.

Podcasting 2.0 is one of the clearest examples of this transformation. Through sats streaming, audiences can send tiny portions of Bitcoin in real time as they listen—literally paying creators by the second. This isn't just tipping or crowdfunding —it's continuous, frictionless appreciation. Each listener becomes part of a self-sustaining micro-economy, rewarding content they truly connect with.

This model strengthens the bond between creator and audience. It transforms passive consumption into active participation. Fans aren't just viewers—they're stakeholders. And creators are free to produce without filtering their voice through corporate sponsors, advertiser guidelines, or opaque algorithms.

By enabling this direct connection, Bitcoin is helping redefine the creative economy around authenticity, trust, and freedom —replacing extractive models with ecosystems where value is earned transparently and relationships matter more than metrics.

Democratization of Innovation

Bitcoin is ushering in a paradigm shift—one that revives personal agency and reclaims the creative power long suppressed by gatekeepers, legacy institutions, and bureaucratic red tape. In the old system, innovation was gated behind connections, credentials, or capital. You had to ask for permission—apply, pitch, fundraise, wait.

That era is ending.

In the Bitcoin ecosystem, the tools to build and share are available to anyone. Open-source protocols, decentralized platforms, and global access mean that if you have a good idea and the drive to pursue it, you don't need approval to get started. The playing field is finally being leveled.

Here, innovation is judged by usefulness and vision—not by resumes or social status. Brilliance is measured by merit, not access. Whether you're a coder in Ghana, an artist in Argentina, or an educator in rural America, you now have the means to contribute meaningfully to systems that shape the future.

This is what real democratization looks like. It's not just about voting once every few years—it's about participating in a continuous, living process of building solutions that matter.

Bitcoin invites individuals to step into that process—not as consumers waiting to be served, but as creators rewriting the rules.

No boardroom. No gatekeeper. Just you, your ideas, and a network that welcomes anyone bold enough to build.

Ripple Effects Across Industries

Bitcoin's disruptive force is rippling across industries—reshaping how we think about communication, learning, health, and finance. What began as a breakthrough in digital money has become a catalyst for rethinking entrenched systems everywhere.

In media, decentralized platforms are giving journalists a way to publish without fear of censorship or editorial interference. No more appeasing advertisers or filtering truth through corporate interests. Writers can now reach global audiences directly, protected by open protocols and sustained by community support—not corporate funding.

In education, Bitcoin-backed initiatives are emerging to serve those left behind by traditional institutions. These platforms emphasize critical thinking, economic literacy, and open access—empowering students who've been underserved, overlooked, or priced out of opportunity. Instead of conformity and debt, they offer knowledge and autonomy.

Healthcare is also feeling the shift. New decentralized applications are being developed to put control over medical data back into the hands of patients. In an era of surveillance medicine and centralized databases, Bitcoin's privacy-first ethos offers a foundation for systems that protect personal information rather than exploit it.

Finance, unsurprisingly, is being shaken to its core. Bitcoin's borderless, transparent design is opening the doors to millions who've been locked out of traditional banking. Whether due to geography, politics, or lack of infrastructure, the unbanked now have a way in—no paperwork required, no approval necessary. All you need is a phone and a few sats.

Each of these transformations has one thing in common: they shift power away from centralized institutions and toward individuals. Bitcoin is not just a financial tool—it's a platform for redefining how freedom, access, and trust are distributed across every sector of society.

Cultivating a Culture of Self-Reliance

The impact of Bitcoin reaches far beyond financial systems or industry-specific innovation—it's reshaping culture itself. As individuals reclaim agency from centralized authorities, a new ethos is taking root—one grounded in self-reliance, mutual respect, and creative independence.

Bitcoin empowers people to build without waiting for approval, to transact without permission, and to collaborate without coercion. That shift rewires how we think about power. It replaces dependency with personal responsibility and transforms consumers into contributors. In this culture, people aren't just opting out of broken systems—they're building better ones in their place.

This change fosters a more collaborative, less extractive environment. Instead of competing for limited resources handed down by gatekeepers, Bitcoin encourages peer-to-peer engagement. Diverse voices are not just welcomed—they're essential. The strength of the system lies in its openness to ideas from every corner of the world, not just the centers of power.

When communities are built around these principles, they tend to be more adaptable, inclusive, and resilient. They grow not through top-down mandates, but through voluntary cooperation and shared vision. People contribute because they believe in the mission—not because they're forced to comply.

This is what a culture of self-reliance looks like: not isolation, but empowerment. Not rugged individualism for its own sake, but interdependence rooted in freedom, dignity, and the ability to create change from the ground up.

Redefining Creator and Consumer Interaction

In the emerging Bitcoin economy, the old boundaries between creator and consumer are fading. What once required layers of intermediaries—publishers, studios, distributors—is now handled peer-to-peer. Decentralized networks are dismantling the gatekeeping structures that once filtered who got to create, who got to speak, and who got paid.

Today, those who produce value can connect directly with those who appreciate it. The result is more than just efficient—it's intimate and genuine. Audiences aren't passive viewers or listeners—they're participants, supporters, even collaborators. And creators are free to prioritize purpose over metrics, quality over virality, and authenticity over commercial conformity.

This new interaction model fosters a more attentive and loyal audience—one that supports content not because it's trending, but because it resonates. In return, creators are liberated from chasing mass appeal and can focus on making meaningful work that reflects their values.

Now imagine what happens when this mindset becomes widespread—when innovation is seen not as a product to be sold, but as a shared process of creation. In this landscape, people aren't just spectators in a digital economy—they're active nodes in a living network fueled by curiosity, creativity, and shared intent.

This is what Bitcoin helps unlock. It provides the infrastructure for a more inclusive, purpose-driven ecosystem —one that values human potential over institutional control. Artists, developers, entrepreneurs, and thinkers can now work on their own terms, unburdened by the approval of legacy systems designed to extract rather than empower.

Growth in this environment is limited only by imagination. And for those ready to explore it, Bitcoin offers more than a new way to transact—it offers a new way to build, connect, and create.

Reflecting on Your Role

Take a moment to consider your place in this evolving landscape. Permissionless innovation isn't just for coders and entrepreneurs—it's for anyone willing to build, contribute, or support ideas rooted in freedom and fairness. You don't need a tech background to participate. You simply need a willingness to step outside the confines of legacy systems and imagine what's possible.

What can you create or support that reflects your values? How can your unique skills—whether technical, artistic, educational, or organizational—contribute to a future where human connection and self-determination take priority over profit margins and corporate control?

This isn't just about adopting new tools—it's about reclaiming agency over your time, your energy, and your voice. It's about carving out a space where creativity thrives without fear, where collaboration replaces competition, and where innovation is a natural extension of personal freedom.

In this vision of the future, your role matters. You're not on the sidelines. You're part of a movement that celebrates authenticity, amplifies diverse voices, and invites all of us to build something better—together.

Building a World You Want to Live In

Bitcoin is not merely a rebellion against the status quo—it is an act of creation. It's not just about escaping the grip of outdated systems; it's about building something better in their place. You're not here to patch up the old world. You're here to replace it with a new one—designed around freedom, fairness, and shared human values.

Creation trumps protest. Instead of only pointing out the flaws in existing institutions, Bitcoin invites us to imagine and construct a reality where money serves people—not the other way around. It asks us not just to exit a broken system, but to take responsibility for shaping what comes next.

This shift—from escape to creation—is foundational. Personal sovereignty, when embraced at scale, becomes community transformation. When individuals take control of their financial lives, they build stronger families and support networks. These networks become the scaffolding for resilient, values-driven economies. As more people adopt Bitcoin, the impact compounds. We don't just empower individuals—we strengthen entire communities.

Some critics claim that institutional adoption of Bitcoin betrays its original mission. They see collaboration with legacy systems as compromise. But Bitcoin was never designed to be exclusive—it was designed to be unbreakable. It welcomes skeptics, cynics, corporations, and even adversaries. That's not a flaw; that's the point. Its openness is what proves its strength. Even when institutions adopt Bitcoin for their own reasons, they validate its core principles: decentralization, transparency, and incorruptibility.

And still—those who adopt early benefit the most. The future is already taking shape, and those who understand Bitcoin now are laying the foundation for a new economic paradigm. When institutions finally catch up, early adopters will already be leading. This is not about hype. It's about vision. It's about building something that lasts.

Your role in this unfolding story is significant. You're not just a cog in the machine—you're a node in a vast, decentralized network of change. Opting into Bitcoin isn't just about side-stepping inflation or government overreach. It's about building a future where autonomy and empowerment aren't fringe ideas—they're the standard.

This isn't just a financial revolution. It's a cultural one. By choosing Bitcoin, you're joining a global movement that prioritizes dignity over control, truth over manipulation, and cooperation over coercion. You're aligning yourself with a vision of prosperity that includes everyone, not just those at the top.

And this alignment has real consequences. As people opt into Bitcoin and opt out of fiat dependence, they start building shared infrastructure—networks rooted in trust, mutual aid, and long-term thinking. These aren't pipe dreams. These are real systems, growing every day, supported by real people.

Bitcoin doesn't just impact individual lives. It reshapes communities, challenges nation-states, and forces global institutions to reckon with a new kind of power—one they can't inflate, censor, or control. This isn't just rebellion. It's renaissance.

So, what does that mean for you?

It means stepping into your power as a builder—not just someone who critiques the world, but someone who creates a better one. Whether you're adopting Bitcoin, supporting open-source projects, or educating others, you are part of this. You are helping build a world worth living in.

Reflect on what that looks like for you. What can you build? What can you support? What conversations can you start? The ripple effects are real—and they begin with you.

True change doesn't start with grand gestures. It starts with one brave choice, made over and over again. It starts with people like you, choosing freedom over fear, intention over convenience, and creation over complacency.

Every decision made with awareness—every sat stacked with purpose—contributes to something greater. A world where wealth is measured not just in numbers, but in meaning. Where prosperity includes purpose. And where freedom isn't granted—it's claimed.

So, as we transition into the next chapter, ask yourself:

What kind of world do you want to live in?

And what are you willing to build to make it real?

CHAPTER 9
START TODAY OR STAY STUCK

"The best time to plant a tree was 20 years ago. The second-best time is now."

— CHINESE PROVERB

Stop Waiting for Permission

You stand at a crossroads—not in theory, but in your real, daily life. The world around you encourages you to stay where it's comfortable, where routines are familiar and systems feel unshakable. But here's the truth: no one is coming to give you permission to change. There's no invitation, no ceremonial ribbon-cutting for personal sovereignty. The world, with its governments, employers, and financial institutions, isn't built to prioritize your autonomy. Not because it's malicious—because it runs on inertia. It survives by keeping you in your place.

This isn't about waiting for approval. You don't need anyone's blessing to choose freedom.

That's the beauty of Bitcoin—it's a self-issued passport to independence. It doesn't ask for validation. It declares, *I'm done waiting.* It's not about rage or rebellion. It's about stepping aside from a system that no longer serves you and choosing a path aligned with your own vision.

But make no mistake: the window is narrowing. The early adopter phase is ending. Every day, the terrain changes as institutions, corporations, and governments begin to stake their claim in Bitcoin. The quiet, open frontier will soon become crowded with complexity. What feels accessible now may become gated later. This is your chance to move before the world catches on.

The decision to engage with Bitcoin is not about being anti-establishment—it's about being *pro-you.* It's not a protest sign. It's a personal vow. A quiet revolution that begins with a simple step.

Yes, it's unfamiliar terrain. There's no detailed map, no guaranteed outcome. But waiting for the perfect moment only ensures one thing: you'll still be waiting. Progress beats perfection every time. Each small action builds momentum. Confidence is earned through motion, not contemplation.

Picture yourself at the edge of possibility—one foot planted in the familiar, the other stretching toward something uncertain but deeply necessary. That first step is everything. It's where ideas become action. Where potential becomes practice. And where your future begins—not when someone says it's okay, but when you decide it's time.

Reflection Exercise

Take a moment to reflect on what has held you back so far. Is it fear of the unknown? A hesitation to make mistakes? Write down your thoughts and consider how they've shaped your financial decisions until now. Then, imagine what taking that first step might look like—perhaps it's setting aside a small amount to invest, or simply committing to learning more about Bitcoin's potential. Whatever it is, embrace the clarity you gain and let it move you forward—today.

This journey isn't about radical transformation overnight; it's about steady progress over time. And the best part? You're not walking it alone. There's a global community—of thinkers, doers, builders, and believers—ready to share insights and support your growth along the way.

By choosing Bitcoin, you're opting into a system built on transparency and fairness—one that values autonomy over control, and empowerment over dependence. It's a chance to redefine wealth on your terms, and to build a life aligned with your values and vision for the future.

As you stand at this crossroads, remember: the power to shape your path lies with you—not with society, not with circumstance, not with outdated expectations. This is your invitation to grow, to break free from the past, and to boldly step into a world of new possibilities.

So, take that first step—whether it's buying your first few sats or deepening your understanding of the Bitcoin network. Because only those who venture beyond the limits of familiarity discover the new horizons waiting just beyond sight.

And as you continue on your path toward financial sovereignty and self-discovery, keep this truth close:

- Every decision teaches you something.
- Every challenge strengthens you.
- Every win builds momentum.

You already hold everything you need—not just to survive, but to thrive.

- Empowered by choice.
- Guided by conviction.
- Fueled by courage.
- Sustained by vision.
- Transformed through action.
- Fulfilled through intention.

And ultimately, defined by the life you choose to live:

- Fully. Freely. Authentically. Unapologetically.
- With clarity. With courage. With purpose.
- On your terms.

IIow to Start — Safely and Simply

Starting with Bitcoin doesn't require a grand leap—it begins with a small, intentional step. This isn't a lottery ticket or a get-rich-quick scheme. It's a commitment to your future self, and like any commitment, it deserves thoughtful planning.

Begin with an amount you can afford to forget about for a while—money you won't need next month or even next year. Let it sit. Let it ride. Treat it as a long-term experiment in patience, discipline, and conviction. Bitcoin is volatile by nature. The early ride can be emotional. But letting your investment rest—untouched and unbothered—gives you time to adjust and build confidence in the process.

Stay away from the noise. Margin, leverage, and hype-fueled slogans are the siren songs that lure newcomers into unnecessary risk. These tools can amplify profits—but they can also wipe out your holdings in a heartbeat. Bitcoin isn't about gambling. It's about long-term, durable growth. Resist the pressure to "go big or go home." Instead, stay grounded. Protect your capital. The goal here isn't thrills—it's freedom.

If and when you decide to sell, be aware of the tax implications. In many jurisdictions, selling Bitcoin triggers capital gains taxes. If you're not prepared, a surprise tax bill can eat into your returns. This is one reason why HODLing—*holding on for dear life*—often makes sense not just emotionally, but financially. Always check your local tax rules before executing any trades that could impact your portfolio.

Security is non-negotiable. One of the safest starting points is collaborative custody—a model that balances autonomy with peace of mind. Services like Unchained or Casa allow you to hold keys while also involving trusted cosigners. This removes single points of failure and adds layers of protection from both hacks and mistakes. You maintain control without carrying the full burden alone.

Eventually, you may choose to move toward full custody. But don't rush it. Educate yourself first. Learn how wallets work. Understand how to create backups. Think through inheritance planning. These details matter—and skipping them could cost you. Take your time. The learning curve may feel steep, but it's one of the most empowering financial skills you'll ever develop.

Getting started with Bitcoin safely isn't about mastering everything on day one. It's about building a foundation—step by step—with clarity, patience, and care. The sooner you begin, the sooner you grow.

Learn More, Trust Less

In the world of Bitcoin, blind trust is a liability. While traditional finance often encourages deference to experts, Bitcoin demands something different: radical responsibility. You're not just a participant—you're the custodian of your own financial future.

That means headlines, influencers, and flashy narratives shouldn't be your compass. Market crashes and explosive rallies will dominate the news cycle, but your most reliable ally isn't hype—it's discernment. Build your understanding through a wide range of perspectives, not just those that reinforce your existing beliefs. In this space, verification matters more than reputation.

Finding reliable sources can feel like trying to tune into a signal buried in static. Start with voices known for clarity and depth. *The Bitcoin Standard* lays a strong foundation. Podcasts like *What Bitcoin Did* offer layered, thoughtful conversations beyond the surface. Seek out educators who filter out noise and focus on principles. And don't overlook real-world connection—Bitcoin meetups can offer genuine conversations and shared learning far beyond what you'll find online.

Bitcoin rewards ongoing curiosity. The space evolves fast, and staying relevant requires lifelong learning. The more you know, the clearer things become—and the more naturally conviction follows. What may begin as a collection of abstract ideas will become a practical framework you can apply to your life and finances.

Even owning a small amount of Bitcoin changes your relationship to money. Suddenly, something that once felt distant becomes personal. It's no longer theoretical—you're part of it. And that shift opens the door to a deeper understanding. It's not just "skin in the game," it's a direct connection to innovation and autonomy.

Bitcoin is an invitation to rethink the nature of money, power, and freedom. It challenges assumptions and pushes you to explore ideas most people never question. There are no shortcuts here—just a path of active inquiry, reflection, and growth.

No source, including this book, should be accepted blindly. Take what's useful and test it. Compare, contrast, and challenge your assumptions. Real conviction doesn't come from following—it comes from building your own conclusions through informed exploration.

The modern world doesn't suffer from a lack of information —it suffers from an overload of it. Learning how to separate signal from noise is an essential skill, especially in Bitcoin. You're not expected to know everything at once. What matters is steady progress—learning how to ask better questions and make more deliberate decisions.

Conviction doesn't arrive all at once. It grows from experience. Each decision to engage, experiment, or study helps build a foundation that's difficult to shake.

This mindset shift—from passive consumption to proactive engagement—extends far beyond Bitcoin. It teaches you how to think critically, act intentionally, and take control of your life with clarity.

You don't need permission. You don't need a roadmap. You need curiosity, a willingness to learn, and the courage to keep going. This is how real freedom begins—not with certainty, but with commitment to learning and the confidence to move forward one decision at a time.

The Life on the Other Side

You've left the noise behind. The endless signs promising riches, shortcuts, and the illusion of stability are fading in the rearview mirror. Ahead is a new kind of journey—not paved with guarantees, but guided by clarity and conviction.

This is the shift Bitcoin offers: from external anxiety to internal certainty, from financial confusion to focused intent. It's not about rebellion for its own sake—it's about crafting a future that feels coherent, meaningful, and fully yours.

Where once your attention was pulled in every direction, now it narrows with purpose. Doubt and instability shrink to background noise, replaced by the steady realization that you are at the helm. The journey ahead may be uncharted, but it's yours to shape—with sharper focus and the confidence that comes from choosing autonomy over dependence.

Planning For the Future with Bitcoin

Bitcoin is more than a stabilizing force—it's a catalyst that reshapes how you envision, strategize, and plan for the future. It invites you to think not in weeks or quarters, but in decades and lifetimes. You're no longer sprinting to keep pace with volatile markets or chasing fleeting gains. Instead, you begin building a durable foundation, guided by conviction and long-term foresight.

Saving in Bitcoin isn't about flashy wealth or short-term thrills. It's about resilience—protecting your time and energy from the corrosive effects of inflation and monetary manipulation. You choose it not for extravagance, but for its power to preserve and grow value across generations.

This isn't just financial planning—it's legacy building. You're laying roots meant to nourish a future that extends beyond your own lifetime. Bitcoin becomes a compass, not just pointing toward wealth, but guiding you toward a life of purpose, clarity, and autonomy—an inheritance of authenticity for those who follow in your path.

Bitcoin as a Guiding Compass

In this analogy, Bitcoin becomes a compass—one that points not to a destination of instant riches, but to a life that resonates with your deepest values. It's not a lottery ticket; it's a finely crafted tool for alignment, one that helps you build a life in harmony with your true self.

As you walk this path at your own pace, the journey itself becomes the reward. True wealth reveals itself not just in numbers, but in autonomy, authenticity, and fulfillment.

Each choice you make is a step toward sovereignty—a declaration that your life is yours to design, not dictated by systems built to serve others. There is no better moment than now to claim that power. The road ahead is open and waiting, unfolding with possibility at every turn.

Embracing the Future Today

This isn't about waiting for perfect conditions or for someone else's permission. It's about realizing the future you envision is yours to shape—one intentional decision at a time. That first step, even if cloaked in uncertainty, is the most important move you'll make. It's the cornerstone of a new life, setting the foundation for freedom, fulfillment, and sovereignty.

Throughout this chapter, we've explored what it means to live on the other side of conventional finance—to shift from anxiety to confidence, from chasing short-term gains to embracing long-term vision. We've seen how Bitcoin is more than a digital asset; it's a compass and a catalyst, guiding you toward a life defined by autonomy, clarity, and purpose.

Transitioning to Practical Steps

As we prepare to close this journey, the path forward becomes clearer. What lies ahead isn't just theory or philosophy—it's the practical work of building your new financial reality. From here, the focus shifts to concrete strategies, tools, and decisions that empower you to take full ownership of your future.

This process goes far beyond simply "making money." It's about crafting a life with intention, one aligned with your values and driven by purpose. Each step is not just about wealth—it's about meaning, about discovering what truly matters and shaping your life around it.

So, carry this with you: The future isn't something to daydream about or wait for. It's something you create—one choice at a time—with clarity, courage, and conviction.

CHAPTER 10
VISUAL PROOF – BITCOIN VS. THE SYSTEM

S ometimes, words aren't enough. We've explored how fiat systems quietly rob you of time, purchasing power, and freedom—while Bitcoin offers a way out. But for those still unsure, sometimes a chart hits harder than any paragraph ever could.

The visuals in this chapter strip away the noise and expose the truth. You'll see how fiat currencies collapse, how the cost of living has outpaced wages, how the money printer distorts reality, and how Bitcoin quietly grows in strength while the system decays. These aren't just charts—they're receipts. They are proof that Bitcoin is not a theory, not a phase, and not just an investment. It's a rebellion. And it's working.

Each image is paired with a short explanation. Share them, save them, question them. Just don't ignore them.

Chart 1: Global Fiat Collapses and Systemic Breakdowns (1923–2021)

(Visual timeline of currency failures and institutional shocks)

"You say you want a revolution... "

— JOHN LENNON

This chart should end the debate.

From Weimar Germany to Lebanon and Argentina, fiat currencies have a 100% failure rate when left unchecked. Politicians print, people suffer, and paper burns. These aren't ancient events—they're happening now.

Show this chart to your financial advisor and ask: *If fiat collapses this often, why should I trust it over Bitcoin?*

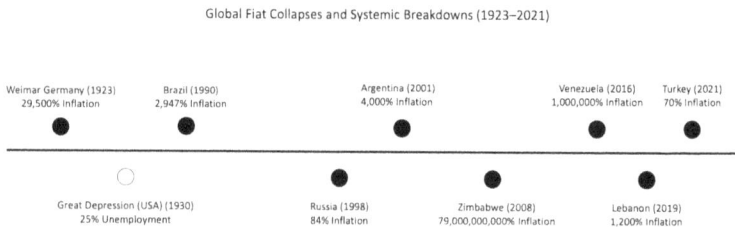

Global Fiat Collapses and Systemic Breakdowns (1923–2021)

Weimar Germany (1923) 29,500% Inflation · Brazil (1990) 2,947% Inflation · Argentina (2001) 4,000% Inflation · Venezuela (2016) 1,000,000% Inflation · Turkey (2021) 70% Inflation

Great Depression (USA) (1930) 25% Unemployment · Russia (1998) 84% Inflation · Zimbabwe (2008) 79,000,000,000% Inflation · Lebanon (2019) 1,200% Inflation

Chart 2: Wages vs. Cost of Living (U.S.)

You're not imagining it.

This chart shows exactly why so many people feel like they're working harder and getting less. Wages have stagnated while the cost of essentials—housing, healthcare, education—has exploded. The system isn't broken. It's rigged.

This isn't just economics—it's theft with a time delay.

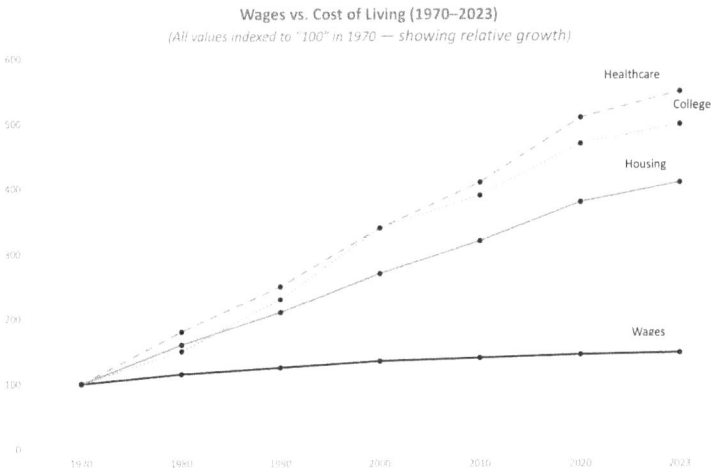

Wages vs. Cost of Living (1970–2023)
(All values indexed to "100" in 1970 — showing relative growth)

Chart 3: M2 Money Supply Expansion (2008–2023)

This is the money printer.

Every surge in this chart represents newly created dollars injected into the system—diluting yours. After 2008, they told you it was necessary. After 2020, they told you it was stimulus. But the more they print, the less your money is worth.

Bitcoin doesn't have a printer. That's the point.

M2 Money Supply Growth (2008–2023)
Measured in trillions of U.S. dollars (M2 supply)

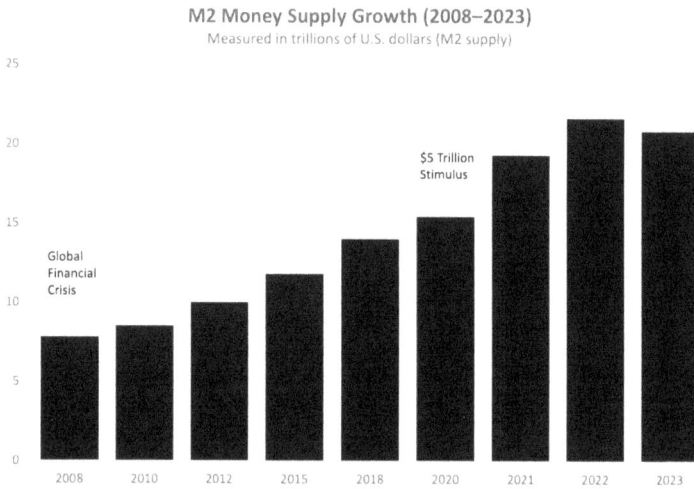

Chart 4: Bitcoin vs. Fiat Money Supply (Halving Comparison)

One gets harder. One gets easier.

As governments crank up the printing press, Bitcoin does the opposite—its supply gets cut in half every four years. This chart compares Bitcoin's engineered scarcity to fiat's engineered inflation. Guess which one wins long-term?

This is what discipline looks like in code.

Bitcoin Shrinks While Fiat Explodes

Money supply vs. Bitcoin issuance by halving cycle (2009–2024)

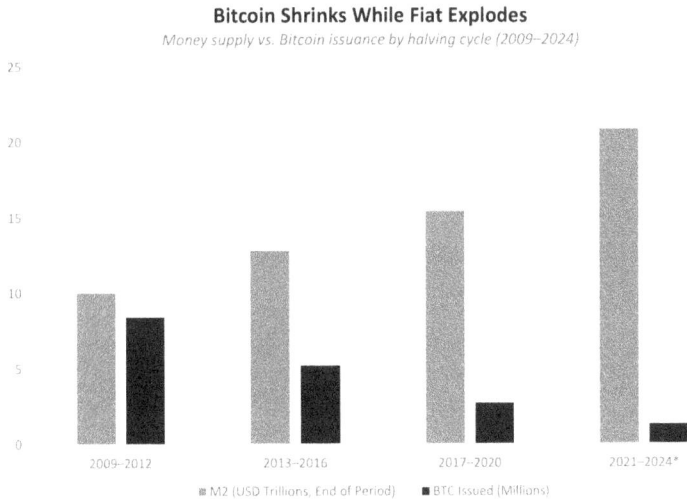

M2 (USD Trillions, End of Period)   ■ BTC Issued (Millions)

Chart 5: DCA vs. Trading vs. Fiat Saving vs. S&P 500

"You don't need to be a revolutionary. Just don't sell your Bitcoin."

— MICHAEL SAYLOR

Simple wins.

This chart shows what happens when you just dollar-cost average into Bitcoin—no trading, no timing, no stress. It outperforms fiat savings, altcoin gamblers, and even the stock market. Time in the market beats timing the market—but with Bitcoin, the gap is staggering.

You don't need to be a genius. You just need conviction.

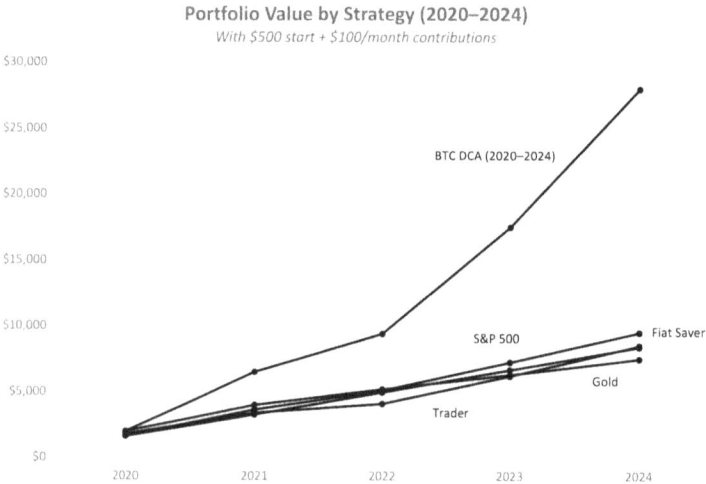

Portfolio Value by Strategy (2020–2024)
With $500 start + $100/month contributions

- BTC DCA (2020–2024)
- S&P 500
- Fiat Saver
- Gold
- Trader

Chart 6: Internet Adoption vs. Bitcoin Adoption Curve

"We're the future, your future."

— SEX PISTOLS, *GOD SAVE THE QUEEN*

It's still early.

This chart overlays Bitcoin's adoption curve with the rise of the internet—and it shows we're not late. If Bitcoin follows a similar path, most of the world hasn't joined yet. That means the biggest gains—and the biggest shifts—are still ahead.

You're not behind. You're just in before the crowd knows it.

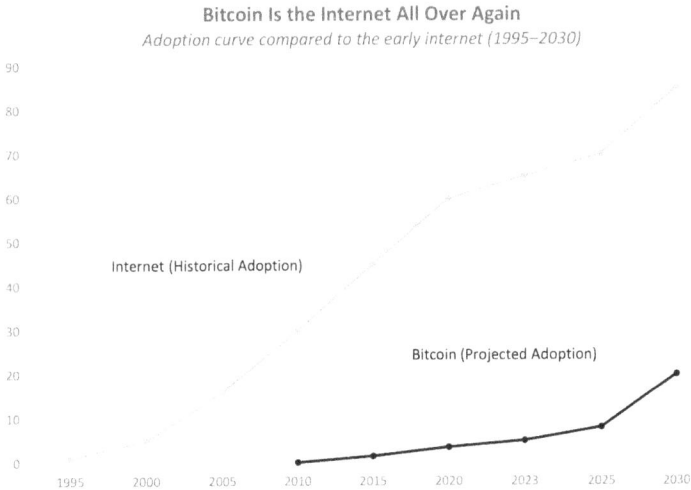

Bitcoin Is the Internet All Over Again
Adoption curve compared to the early internet (1995–2030)

Internet (Historical Adoption)

Bitcoin (Projected Adoption)

Chart 7: Platform Censorship vs. Bitcoin's Censorship Resistance

They can freeze your money. Bitcoin can't.

This chart compares frozen accounts, banned platforms, and digital payment blocks—all reminders that your money isn't really yours in the fiat system. With Bitcoin, no one can stop a valid transaction. No bank manager. No government. No algorithm.

Ask your advisor: *Can my bank say no to my money?* Bitcoin doesn't.

Permissioned Platforms vs. Permissionless Money
Estimated user-level censorship incidents (based on public reports)

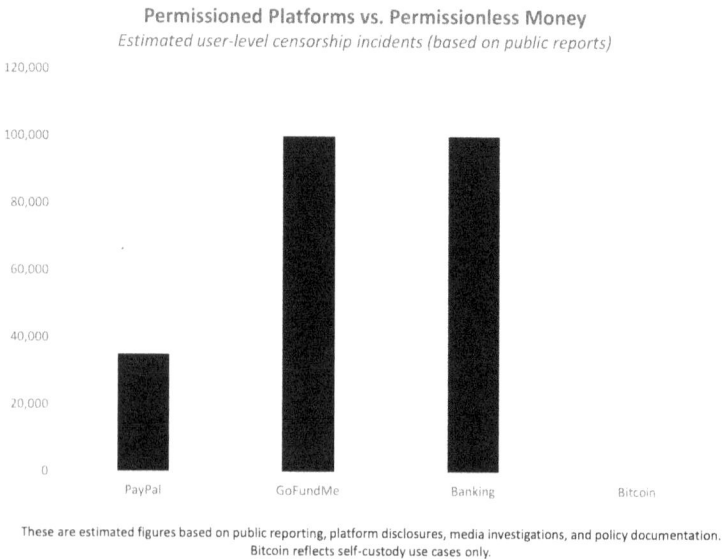

These are estimated figures based on public reporting, platform disclosures, media investigations, and policy documentation. Bitcoin reflects self-custody use cases only.

Chart 8: Bitcoin vs. Traditional Assets – Cumulative Returns

This is what outperformance looks like.

Bitcoin doesn't just beat traditional assets—it laps them. This chart compares cumulative 5-year and 10-year returns across Bitcoin, the stock market, gold, and real estate. Even scaled down, Bitcoin leaves everything in the dust.

Show this to your advisor and ask: Why aren't they telling you about this?

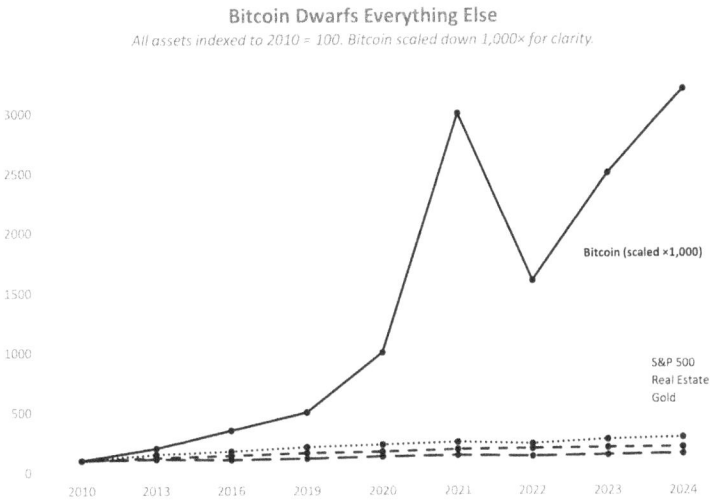

Bitcoin Dwarfs Everything Else
All assets indexed to 2010 = 100. Bitcoin scaled down 1,000× for clarity.

Chart 9: Bitcoin in Collapsing Fiat Economies

When local currencies collapse, Bitcoin doesn't.

This chart compares Bitcoin's performance against inflation in countries like Argentina, Lebanon, and Nigeria—places where the fiat system has failed hard. In every case, Bitcoin protected more value than the local currency.

It's not just theory. It's already saving people—just not the ones your bank is watching.

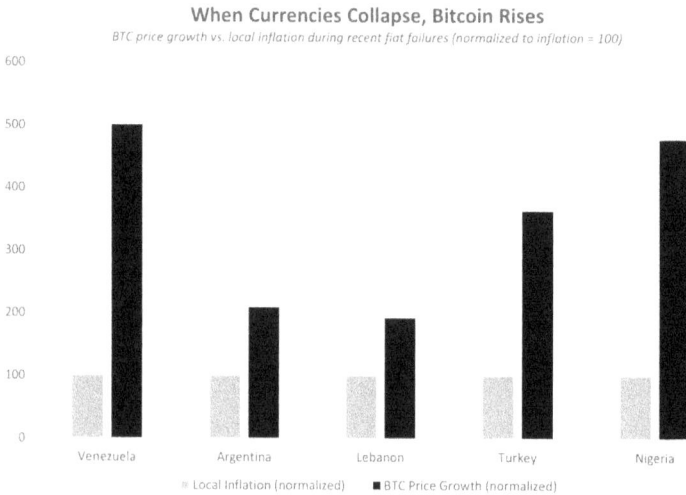

When Currencies Collapse, Bitcoin Rises
BTC price growth vs. local inflation during recent fiat failures (normalized to inflation = 100)

Local Inflation (normalized) ■ BTC Price Growth (normalized)

Chart 10: Bitcoin vs. USD Drawdowns (Volatility vs. Fiat Decay)

"Volatility is a prerequisite to performance."

— JACK MALLERS

Yes, Bitcoin crashes. But fiat never recovers.

This chart shows Bitcoin's biggest yearly drawdowns next to the quiet, relentless erosion of the U.S. dollar. Bitcoin's volatility is temporary. Fiat's decay is permanent. Which would you rather ride out?

If your advisor says Bitcoin is "too volatile," ask: *What do you call guaranteed loss?*

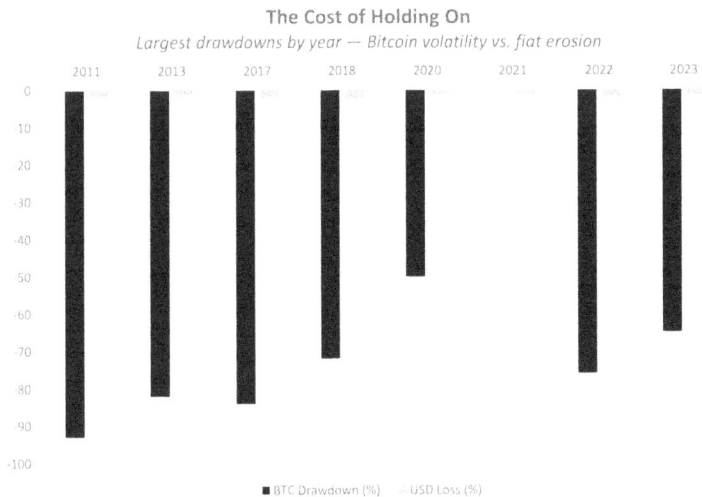

The Cost of Holding On
Largest drawdowns by year — Bitcoin volatility vs. fiat erosion

Chart 11: Custody Risk Spectrum

Where you keep your Bitcoin is everything.

This chart shows the spectrum of custody—from self-sovereignty to total risk. Self-custody puts you in control. Custodians, exchanges, and ETFs put your future in someone else's hands. Guess which side regulators prefer.

This isn't just storage. It's freedom or permission.

Bitcoin Custody Risk Spectrum
Not your keys, not your coins.

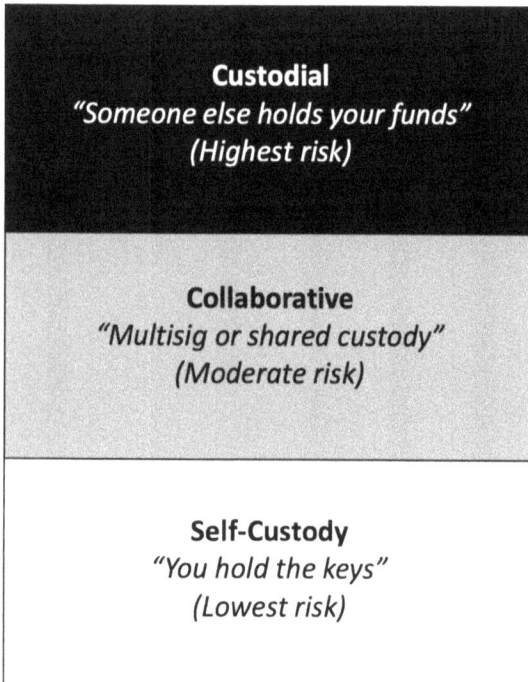

Custodial
"Someone else holds your funds"
(Highest risk)

Collaborative
"Multisig or shared custody"
(Moderate risk)

Self-Custody
"You hold the keys"
(Lowest risk)

Chart 12: Bitcoin vs. Traditional Assets (2024 Snapshot)

"To be truly radical is to make hope possible, rather than despair convincing."

— RAYMOND WILLIAMS

This is the end of the argument.

Over both 5 and 10 years, Bitcoin has crushed every traditional asset class—stocks, gold, real estate. This isn't a bubble. It's what happens when you buy something truly scarce in a world drowning in printed money.

If your advisor isn't showing you this chart, ask them why.

Cumulative Returns: Bitcoin vs. Traditional Assets
Performance from mid-2014 and mid-2019 to 2024

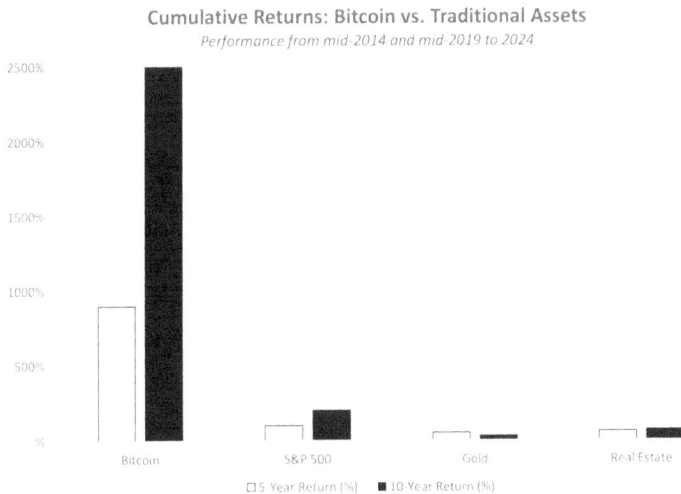

You've seen the data. These charts don't rely on hype—they reveal what the system wants you to overlook. If your advisor, banker, or favorite pundit can't explain them, maybe it's time to stop asking for permission. The numbers are already telling you what to do.

CONCLUSION: THE POWER TO WALK AWAY

As we close this final chapter, take a moment to reflect on the journey we've taken together. What began as frustration with a system that quietly siphons your time, your energy, and your wealth has become something far more powerful: a realization that you don't have to play their game anymore.

Bitcoin is your way out. Not just a new kind of money, but a new kind of power—one that puts you in control. It's a tool for reclaiming sovereignty, aligning your financial life with your values, and opting out of systems that were never built with your freedom in mind.

In a world of infinite fiat, Bitcoin offers hard limits. In a world of surveillance and control, it offers privacy and permissionlessness. And in a world where profit is prioritized over people, it gives you the ultimate leverage: the ability to say "no." To debt. To inflation. To broken promises and economic gaslighting. That's what makes Bitcoin *F*ck You Money*—not because it's loud or aggressive, but because it's quietly, permanently yours.

The steps to get there don't need to be dramatic. You don't need to go all in. You just need to start—learn, stack, and take custody. Let conviction grow through knowledge. Let your actions become bolder as your understanding deepens. This is a process of unlearning dependence and rediscovering agency.

The truth is, you won't get an engraved invitation to exit the system. You have to choose it. And that choice, when made with intention, becomes a declaration: *I won't be owned. I won't be extracted from. I choose freedom instead.*

So, here's your call to action: Don't wait for the stars to align. They won't. Start now—small if you must, but start. Every sat you stack, every key you hold, every idea you question is a step toward independence.

Picture your life free from the treadmill of debt and the creeping erosion of your purchasing power. Imagine building a future that reflects your values, not someone else's agenda. That future isn't a fantasy—it's available right now, and Bitcoin is the engine that can take you there.

Thank you for getting this far. That alone shows strength—because it takes guts to look beyond the familiar, to challenge what you've been told, and to carve your own path. You are not a passive player in this story. You are the author.

And now you have the pen.

So, take the next step with clarity and confidence. You don't need to burn it all down. You just need to walk away—one decision, one sat, one block at a time.

That's F*ck You Money. And it's yours, if you want it.

.

RESOURCES FOR BUILDING CONVICTION AND TAKING ACTION

Many of the resources listed here are ones I've personally used—and they've directly inspired the writing of this book. My goal isn't to tell you what to think, but to point you toward the people, platforms, and tools that helped shape my own understanding. What you do with them is up to you. Whether you're here to learn, build, connect, or take action, these are some of the most reliable and empowering places to start. Scan the QR codes, follow your curiosity, and stay sharp. Bitcoin rewards those who take responsibility and never stop learning.

The Bitcoin Standard – Saifedean Ammous

This foundational book makes the case for Bitcoin as a return to sound money. It traces the history of monetary systems and explains why fiat currencies are prone to inflation and manipulation, while Bitcoin's fixed supply makes it a reliable store of value in the digital age.

Bitcoin Magazine

Founded in 2012, Bitcoin Magazine is one of the most trusted and longest-standing publications covering Bitcoin development, policy, culture, and market trends. It's a great ongoing source for staying informed.

Bitcoin is Hope – Michael Saylor

A platform featuring interviews, speeches, and resources from Michael Saylor. It focuses on how Bitcoin empowers individuals as a secure savings tool, particularly in inflationary or unstable economic environments.

The 'What is Money?' Show – Robert Breedlove

A podcast that takes a philosophical and historical approach to understanding money, power, and human freedom. Breedlove interviews economists, historians, and Bitcoin thinkers to explore how Bitcoin fits into the bigger picture.

Talking Bitcoin / Coin Stories – Natalie Brunell

Natalie Brunell interviews prominent voices in Bitcoin, exploring its implications for personal finance, geopolitics, and cultural change. Clear, accessible, and inspiring.

Simply Bitcoin

This daily news and commentary platform is designed to help you cut through noise and stay up to date on significant Bitcoin developments. It's ideal for those who want to stay informed but are short on time.

Casa

A self-custody company offering multisig wallets, inheritance solutions, and user-friendly apps. Casa makes advanced Bitcoin security more accessible for individuals and families who want to hold their own keys.

Unchained Capital

A Bitcoin-native financial company offering collaborative custody, Bitcoin-backed loans, and Bitcoin IRAs. Their 2-of-3 vault system allows you to hold two keys while they hold one, balancing autonomy with security and support.

Bitcoin Mentor

A one-on-one coaching service that helps beginners overcome confusion and start their Bitcoin journey with confidence. Emphasis on clarity, custody, and conviction, with a highly personal approach.

The Bitcoin Way

This company offers hands-on training and consulting to help individuals become self-sovereign. Services include privacy coaching, self-custody guidance, and even alternative residency options.

Coinkite

Makers of the COLDCARD hardware wallet, TAPSIGNER, and other high-security Bitcoin tools. Known for their "Don't Trust, Verify" ethos and deep commitment to privacy and personal control.

Bitcoin IRA

A platform that lets U.S. users invest in Bitcoin and other cryptocurrencies inside tax-advantaged retirement accounts. Provides 24/7 trading and integration with regulated custodians.

Ledn

A financial services firm offering Bitcoin savings accounts, Bitcoin-backed loans, and innovative products like B2X and DCA loans. Focused on helping users grow their Bitcoin stack while maintaining custody and liquidity.

Orange Pill App

A social app for Bitcoiners to find meetups, merchants, and other enthusiasts in their local area. Includes Lightning integration and a robust event calendar—ideal for making real-world connections.

REFERENCES

Al Jazeera. (2021). How Lebanon's currency crisis unfolded. https://www.aljazeera.com/economy/2021/7/1/lebanon-crisis-fuel-prices-electricity

Bitcoin.org. (n.d.). Bitcoin issuance schedule and halving explanation. https://bitcoin.org/en/how-it-works

Bitcoin.org. (n.d.). How Bitcoin works – censorship resistance. https://bitcoin.org/en/how-it-works

Bloomberg. (2022, March 15). Global bank account freezes top 100,000. https://www.bloomberg.com/news/articles/2022-03-15/global-bank-account-freezes-top-100-000

Board of Governors of the Federal Reserve System. (2024). M2 money stock (M2SL) [FRED economic data]. https://fred.stlouisfed.org/series/M2SL

Breedlove, R. (n.d.). The number zero and Bitcoin. https://medium.com/@breedlove22/the-number-zero-and-bitcoin-4c05226f62fc

Bureau of Labor Statistics. (n.d.). Labor force statistics from the current population survey. https://www.bls.gov/cps/

Bureau of Labor Statistics. (n.d.). Median usual weekly earnings of full-time wage and salary workers. https://www.bls.gov

Chainalysis. (2024). Crypto adoption in emerging markets. https://www.chainalysis.com/

Chainalysis. (n.d.). What is Bitcoin's price history? https://www.chainalysis.com

Charles Schwab. (n.d.). Why investors fail: Understanding behavioral investing. https://www.schwab.com/learn/story/why-investors-fail

Clark Moody. (n.d.). Bitcoin dashboard – issuance and halving data. https://clarkmoody.com/dashboard/

Coin Center. (2022, February 4). GoFundMe blocks Canadian Freedom Convoy funds. https://www.coincenter.org/gofundme-and-censorship/

Coindesk. (2024). Bitcoin historical price index. https://www.coindesk.com/price/bitcoin/

CoinDesk. (n.d.). Bitcoin price index. https://www.coindesk.com/price/bitcoin/

CoinMarketCap. (2025). Bitcoin historical price data. Retrieved from https://coinmarketcap.com/currencies/bitcoin/historical-data/

Coinrule. (n.d.). HODL vs. trading: Which strategy works best? https://coin rule.com

College Board. (2022). Trends in college pricing and student aid 2022. https:// research.collegeboard.org/trends/college-pricing

Federal Reserve Bank of St. Louis. (2024). U.S. home price index (CSUSHPINSA). https://fred.stlouisfed.org/series/CSUSHPINSA

Federal Reserve Bank of St. Louis. (n.d.). M2 money stock (M2SL). https:// fred.stlouisfed.org/series/M2SL

Federal Reserve Bank of St. Louis. (n.d.). Median sales price of houses sold for the United States. https://fred.stlouisfed.org/series/MSPUS

Friedrich, B. (2022). We are still measuring inflation all wrong. Cato Institute. https://www.cato.org/blog/we-are-still-measuring-inflation-all-wrong-2

GoFundMe. (2022). Freedom Convoy fundraiser removed for violating terms of service. https://www.cnbc.com/2022/02/05/gofundme-takes-down-trucker-fundraiser.html

GoldHub. (2024). Gold price historical data. https://www.gold.org/goldhub/ data/gold-prices

International Monetary Fund. (2016–2019). Venezuela: Staff reports. https:// www.imf.org/en/Countries/VEN

Internet World Stats. (n.d.). Internet growth statistics. https://www.internet worldstats.com/emarketing.htm

Investopedia. (2024). What is the average annual return for the S&P 500? https://www.investopedia.com/ask/answers/042415/what-average-annual-return-sp-500.asp

Investopedia. (2025). Has real estate or the stock market performed better historically? Retrieved from https://www.investopedia.com/ask/answers/ 052015/which-has-performed-better-historically-stock-market-or-real-estate.asp

Investopedia. (n.d.). Weimar Republic hyperinflation. https://www.investope dia.com/terms/w/weimar-republic.asp

Kaiser Family Foundation. (2023). Health spending in the U.S. https://www. kff.org/health-costs/

MacroTrends. (2025). Gold prices - 100 year historical chart. Retrieved from https://www.macrotrends.net/1333/historical-gold-prices-100-year-chart

MacroTrends. (2025). S&P 500 historical annual returns. Retrieved from https://www.macrotrends.net/2526/sp-500-historical-annual-returns

NerdWallet. (2024). Best high-yield online savings accounts. https://www. nerdwallet.com/best/banking/high-yield-online-savings-accounts

PayPal. (2020). Why is my account limited? https://www.paypal.com/us/ smarthelp/article/why-is-my-account-limited-faq1627

Pew Research Center. (2012). The lost decade of the middle class. https:// www.pewresearch.org/social-trends/2012/08/22/the-lost-decade-of-the- middle-class/

S&P Dow Jones Indices. (2024). S&P 500 historical data. https://www. spglobal.com/spdji/en/

Saifedean, A. (2018). The Bitcoin standard: The decentralized alternative to central banking. Wiley.

Saylor, M. (2021). Don't sell your Bitcoin, sell your debt. [Interview or quote, often referenced in talks and online content by Michael Saylor]

Seyffart, J. (n.d.). [Insights and analysis via social media and public appearances].

St. Louis Fed. (2023). The state of U.S. wealth inequality. Federal Reserve Bank of St. Louis. https://www.stlouisfed.org/community-development- research/the-state-of-us-wealth-inequality

Statista. (2022). Inflation rate in Turkey 2002–2022. https://www.statista. com/statistics/263616/inflation-rate-in-turkey/

Statista. (2024). Inflation rate by country 2023–2024. https://www.statista.com/

The Guardian. (2021, October 8). PayPal policies face criticism over vague bans and political bias. https://www.theguardian.com/technology/2021/ oct/08/paypal-bans-criticism

Trading Economics. (n.d.). Argentina inflation rate. https://tradingeconom ics.com/argentina/inflation-cpi

TradingView. (2024). Bitcoin price history. https://www.tradingview.com/

U.S. Bureau of Labor Statistics. (2024). Consumer Price Index (CPI) data. https://www.bls.gov/cpi/

U.S. Census Bureau. (n.d.). Historical income tables: People. https://www. census.gov/data/tables/time-series/demo/income-poverty/historical- income-people.html

What Bitcoin Did. (n.d.). Podcast series hosted by Peter McCormack. https:// www.whatbitcoindid.com/

Woon, W. (2021). Bitcoin adoption curve model. Woo Charts. https:// woocharts.com

World Bank. (2024). Inflation, consumer prices (annual %). https://data. worldbank.org/indicator/FP.CPI.TOTL.ZG

World Bank. (n.d.). Brazil inflation, consumer prices (annual %). https://data. worldbank.org/indicator/FP.CPI.TOTL.ZG?locations=BR

World Bank. (n.d.). Russian Federation inflation, consumer prices (annual %). https://data.worldbank.org/indicator/FP.CPI.TOTL.ZG?locations=RU

World Bank. (n.d.). Zimbabwe inflation, consumer prices (annual %). https://data.worldbank.org/indicator/FP.CPI.TOTL.ZG?locations=ZW

www.ingramcontent.com/pod-product-compliance
Lightning Source LLC
Chambersburg PA
CBHW040926210326
41597CB00030B/5194